The Little Book of Leadership

A collection of insightful and practical business soundbites to help you lead and succeed in today's commercial world.

Contents

The Man in the Arena

'It is not the critic who counts; not the man who points out how the strong man stumbles, or where the doer of deeds could have done them better. The credit belongs to the man who is actually in the arena, whose face is marred by dust and sweat and blood; who strives valiantly; who errs, who comes short again and again, because there is no effort without error and shortcoming; but who does actually strive to do the deeds; who knows great enthusiasms, the great devotions; who spends himself in a worthy cause; who at the best knows in the end the triumph of high achievement, and who at the worst, if he fails, at least fails while daring greatly, so that his place shall never be with those cold and timid souls who neither know victory nor defeat.' —Theodore Roosevelt

To my darling Emily (and our dog, Maggie!) for giving me the space to be the man in the arena, and to my mother and father for raising me in a way that ensured my 'place shall never be with those cold and timid souls who neither know victory nor defeat'.

Dedication

'Gratitude is a powerful catalyst for happiness.

It's the spark that lights a fire of joy in your soul.'

—Amy Collette

I knew someone who caught a throat infection in the summer of 2021. The initial illness subsided, but the person was left with a hoarse voice. A month later, their voice was still not back to normal, so, after a loving nudge from their partner, they booked a telephone appointment with a doctor.

At the end of the appointment, the doctor concluded that there was no need to worry. Due to the origin of the condition being known, the doctor was confident that the hoarseness would naturally resolve. The doctor advised the person to make another appointment in three weeks if it persisted.

Three weeks later and the hoarseness had not gone, so the person telephoned the surgery and spoke to the doctor again. The doctor repeated his previous advice, but added that if the hoarseness did not clear in another three weeks, then an in-person appointment would be required.

Another three weeks passed, and the voice was still not right, so the person followed the doctor's advice and made a physical appointment. A couple of weeks after that, the person found themselves in the doctor's waiting room with the expectation of leaving 30 minutes later with a prescription.

As the appointment progressed, the doctor became visibly more concerned. He finished his examination and steadied himself before saying to the person that they were exhibiting symptoms of lung cancer. The doctor explained that time was now a factor and further tests were needed as a priority.

The doctor booked an emergency chest x-ray and an appointment with an ear, nose and throat consultant. There was an unavoidable four-week wait (the UK was in a pandemic). The person asked how they could access information in the interim and the doctor directed them to the National Health Service (NHS) website.

The person left the doctor, got into their car, and immediately accessed the NHS website. They felt a knot in their stomach when reading that only one in three survive more than a year after diagnosis. Now they understood why the doctor had emphasised that testing was a priority.

The person used the four weeks to ensure that their critical illness cover, insurance policy holders, solicitors and a human resources confidante were all aligned. The person took comfort in knowing their loved ones would be financially secure if the worst outcome was to become a reality.

The day of the x-ray arrived. The entire process was performed with perfect professionalism by a doctor and nurse combo, who provided a polite and underwhelming experience that lasted no more than 15 minutes. The person then drove back to their home feeling a little numb.

A week later and the appointment with the consultant arrived. Having mentally prepared for their worst fears to be confirmed, the journey to the hospital was a strangely calm affair. When your enemy is a disease, then it would seem everything is quite matter of fact.

Once in the hospital, the person soon found the oncology waiting room. The person could tell by the look in the eyes of those already in the waiting room that they (young and old) had already received their bad news and were receiving treatment.

The person's heart broke for them all, and the families and loved ones they might leave behind. He then composed himself as he fought back a huge feeling of sadness and guilt, as he thought of what his early death might do to those he would leave behind.

The person's name was called, and they were shown to a room with a consultant and a nurse. Before anyone could say hello, the person asked, 'Do I have cancer?' The consultant replied, in a very serious tone, that there was no evidence of cancer in the x-rays and the possibility was now remote.

The nurse handed the person a tissue to wipe away any tears of relief. The person did not have tears at this point and so handed it back. A short time later, during the consultation, the person became aware of the nurse wiping her own eyes. When she saw him looking, she explained with a smile that it was rare to give good news, and it always overwhelmed her.

I am sure you have probably suspected that the person in this story was me. The feeling of relief when hearing that my x-rays were clear was immense. I had effectively been given a second chance at life, and it was a sensation that I still cannot put into words.

Nobody in my personal or professional life knew about this at the time.

I wanted to begin this book with this story and use it as a reminder to us all that it is unlikely that you will ever know a person's full story, especially if you only know them in a professional sense. So, be as kind as you can and act with professional integrity, because not everyone gets the good news I did.

This book is dedicated to the families of those who were in the oncology waiting room, and the loved ones that I would have left behind had the consultant given me different news. The profits that are received from this endeavour will be donated to Macmillan Cancer Support in the hope that they might make the journey easier for those who have no option but to travel that frightening path.

Forward

'In order to write about life first you must live it.'

- Ernest Hemingway

My story started with an adventurous childhood, progressed to a carefree youth, and then arrived unapologetically at breakneck speed into an adulthood that was hallmarked by a feeling of contentment when operating within some of the world's most hazardous environments.

My career journey began with a focus on close protection and anti-terrorism. This was a long way from the imaginings of my wonderful parents, who worked so hard to send me to a good school, and then on to one of the country's top universities. But it was very much where my heart lay, and something they both understood I needed to do. This was a joy for a young man who was filled with ideals and testosterone, and I absorbed as much about that stage in my life as I possibly could.

Then, due to a chance encounter in an infamous pub in Aberdeen (Scotland) with a charismatic, if not rather overzealous and perhaps inebriated, oil rig manager, I moved to a career in the offshore energy industry. This allowed me to travel extensively all over the world, from windswept oceans and freezing tundra to claustrophobic jungles and blazing desserts that were so hot they felt more like the surface of the sun than any kind of earthly drilling site.

My career then moved onshore, much to my dismay, and onto management. I had tried to avoid this and 'keep the coveralls' for as long as I could, as I was under the impression it would be mundane (I was mistaken). I soon discovered that the skills I had learnt from evading gangsters in Azerbaijan and narrowly avoiding being kidnapped in the East African dessert were just as applicable in the 'office'. The only difference was that, in my new environment, I was required to develop a different type of situational awareness because the threats were often more difficult to see coming.

Within this book, I have tried to capture as many lessons as I could from every part of my career. You will read about how to lead and when to manage, gain an insight into the cognitive processes that influence our decisions, as well as the importance of engaging those in the workforce so that they work with you, and not against you. But be warned, it won't all be a bed of roses, I will also talk about the darker side of what can go wrong and, as you will read, the devastatingly tragic consequences that can follow.

My hope is that you enjoy this book, and that it plays a part in your own developmental journey. The profits from this book will go to an incredibly valuable charity so thank you for investing, but please do not let that stop you from passing it on to a friend or colleague if you think they may benefit. As much as I believe in MacMillan Cancer Support with my heart and soul, I believe in the potential within people even more (and we all have a role to play in unlocking that).

Chapter One

Leadership, Management & Well-being

'A leader is best when people barely know he exists, when his work is done, his aim fulfilled, they will say: we did it ourselves.'

—Lao Tsu

Dependable, resilient, and competent leadership is a rarity in today's commercial world. This forgotten art is just one of the many management travesties in the corporate world, because it was within that elusive demographic that we found the hallmarks of success.

Developing this aspirational sub-group of exceptional leaders is rarely the product of 'cookie-cutter' programmes. Even the highly prestigious Royal Military Academy Sandhurst, with its robust leadership programme, merely places the individual on the right path. But, whatever path the future leader chooses in their developmental journey, from university to the coalface, they would do well to follow six proven principles which have come to be accepted as axioms of the leadership world:

1. Take ownership: Everything in life becomes easier when you accept that a mistake is only a failure when you blame others for the outcome. When you are enlightened enough to take ownership, then you are in the driving seat of whether you are a failure or a learner.
2. Identify what is important: You can only bring a vision into focus once you have defined what really matters. These values and standards provide lifelong references that keep focus, guide behaviours, and set the stage for the strategic decision-making that sets you apart.
3. Focus on the mission: An effective leader can filter what is urgent from what is important and divert resources to areas that will serve the greatest purpose. This ensures that there is maximum impact on critical path items, and that the 'noise' is dealt with appropriately.
4. Become an active listener: This skill surpasses simply showing an interest, as it is about making the best effort to understand another person's perspective and, in so doing, cultivate a relationship built on mutual trust. This means fighting the urge to answer, and building your credibility by caring.
5. Understanding the power of collaboration: Even when operating at 100% productivity, the outcome will still be far behind a team that shares values-based behaviours and a mutually beneficial mindset. Facilitating self-supporting synergy moves the dial from good to great.
6. Understanding the selflessness of self-care: As an instrument of your own success, it is imperative that you maximise self-

efficiency and ensure that you give yourself the best possible opportunity. This means committing to your physical, mental, and emotional health.

Once a leader is comfortable with the six principles, they can combine their personality, character, knowledge, understanding and experience with their values to produce a contextually relevant style(s) of their own. Sometimes, it helps to consider these styles on a spectrum that begins with 'transactional' and then ends with 'transformational'. These polarised aspects can be defined as:

Transactional (Tra): This is directive and can usually be derived from monetary values. Prevalent in hierarchical organisations that focus on quantitative performance. Although criticised for stifling creativity, many subordinates prefer this kind of well-defined structure and conformity as it leaves them with little doubt about where they stand.

Transformational (Trf): This is largely based upon a connection made on an emotional level, often referred to as a psychological contract. It requires strong role models who communicate a shared vision and unified purpose that empowers and motivates teams and individuals to perform beyond the expectations contained within an employment contract.

So, if we bookend the transactional and transformational approaches as representing the two ends of the leadership spectrum, the requirement for a rudimentary understanding of what lies in between those two points becomes apparent. It is at this point that we can begin to codify the process by sub-dividing the range into six distinct sections, starting with the transactional (Tra) and moving towards transformational (Trf):

1) **Directive (Tra):** An authoritative approach best deployed when rapid results are required. It is tempting for poor leaders to regress into this approach during times of fatigue or stress. Common telltale phrase: 'Do what I tell you...'
2) **Pacesetting (Tra):** Leading by example and challenging others to keep up often motivates, but care must be taken as it can be equally demoralising for those unable to sustain the pace. Common telltale phrase: 'Do what I do...'
3) **Participative (Tra/Trf):** This involves building commitment through engagement in a psychologically safe environment where timely, constructive criticism and challenges are welcomed. Common telltale phrase: 'What do you think...'
4) **Coaching (Trf/Tra):** Helps to develop your team personnel by identifying their strengths and weaknesses, and working to build long-term capabilities, a forward focus, and a healthy team dialogue. Common telltale phrase: 'What could you achieve…'
5) **Affiliative (Trf):** Focuses on identifying and addressing individual and team needs, in the hope the investment will turn into engagement by doing. However, a leader must be aware that a 'hands-off' approach could lead to poor results. Common telltale phrase: 'People come first...'
6) **Visionary (Trf):** A vision and strategy is communicated clearly, but the mission and tactics are left to the team to

prioritise/decide. This can encourage collective strength and be exceptionally effective. Common telltale phrase: 'This is where we are going...'

It would be a mistake to think that all great leaders have been 'codified' in a way that allows the rest of us mere mortals to simply 'hack' our way to success. Leadership often hinges on something far more complex, such as having personnel in pivotal position(s) who possess the ability to use collective beliefs, behaviours, and mindsets to match 'the way we do things' with the task at hand.

This means a leader must also be:

a) **aware** enough to recognise what styles they need to adopt,
b) **humble** enough to studiously develop them, and
c) remain **competent** enough to use them.

Now that the leader understands the basic principles, and the styles by which they can be deployed, they must start to become familiar with behavioural enablers. Recognising the benefits that these psychological catalysts bring to leadership can be the difference between victory and failure.

Leading in a meaningful way, especially within an empathetic world (courtesy of the pandemic), often pivots on iterations of the autonomous, creative, and empowered (ACE) framework (see below). This pragmatic approach aligns with Apple founder, Steve Job's, philosophy, '*It doesn't make sense to hire smart people and tell them what to do; we hire smart people so they can tell us what to do.*'

Autonomy (A): Allows independent action, but with collective protection. An example might be a specialist military unit that is able to conduct itself in whatever manner is appropriate to achieve the mission, but ultimately knows the cavalry is never too far away.

Creativity (C): Facilitates the team to think its way to success without impediment from a restrictive one-size-fits-all prescriptive management function. This engages and focuses the team members whilst ensuring they are personally invested in success, because it is their idea, after all.

Empowerment (E): This lets the team members act on their own volition. This agility requires a rock-solid relationship between the leader and their team that is built upon a mutual understanding based on trust and respect.

However, it takes immense courage for a leader to let go of control, and then invariably defend that approach of the legacy status quo stalwarts that plague the halls of power because of their inability to 'let go'. For those leaders who are brave enough to take that leap of faith, there can be no higher reward than the satisfaction of facilitating their personnel on a growth path to excellence.

Within a high-performing organisation, delegation is essential and encouraged, as it has been proven to build resilience and agility to achieve the vision and mission of the company. It is necessary and encouraged to instil mutual trust throughout the chain of command, and invariably elevates many of those within the organisation from good to great. However, asking others to step out of their core competency and develop their cognitive abilities also carries an inherent risk.

Leaders must, therefore, assess the operational landscape to establish at what degree they can delegate without compromising their own risk tolerance. If this is miscalculated, and a loss occurs, the law (certainly that of the United Kingdom) will generally apportion blame to the leader.

For example, within Section 2 'General duties of employers to their employees' of the Health and Safety at Work etc. Act 1974, subsection 2 paragraph c) states that an employer's duty extends to 'the provision of such information, instruction, training and supervision as is necessary to ensure, so far as is reasonably practicable, the health and safety at work of his employees'.

This requirement is reflected within most organisations' management systems. This means the burden of leadership, in terms of the law, can be thought of as the consequences associated with the delegation of duties. Military parallels can be drawn between mission command (execution) and command responsibility (assurance).

However, if things do not go as planned, we must be careful not to distance ourselves legally and morally by apportioning blame. This type of defence perpetuates a self-serving process of corporate denial. The truth is that the factors that facilitated the event were in place under our oversight, and so a leader must also own them.

Now that we are familiar with the basics, both good and bad, our next port of call should be to look at the importance of integrating authentic values. An empathetic servant leadership style has become very effective in recent times, and this is understandable when we factor in the public's yearning for reassurance on global issues ranging from pandemics to debt crisis to geopolitical instability.

The simple truth is that the success of this approach is completely dependent upon the trust that is in place between leaders and their followers. Anyone who has ever had this bond with their supervisor will testify to the favourable employment conditions (often outside of the remit of a black and white impersonal employment contract) being reflected by them within the workplace with professionalism and productivity. This type of supervisor often achieves the best results.

However, when there is an imbalance between the conditions provided and professionalism received, we can often trace that to a misalignment between values and/ or standards. Someone is not giving back what they are receiving. This means that we can then assume, to some extent, that the standards used to create an outcome will reflect those used during the journey where professional integrity is built.

This level of interdependency demonstrates that values, as well as the standards that enact them, can also be codified. If this is the case, then they can also be 'hacked' to optimise performance. This means that a leader does not necessarily have to have an intimate understanding of their people, just the knowledge and ability to consistently apply the values and standards that their personnel require.

An example of this was shown by the late Nelson Mandela, one of the greatest leaders of modern times. Mandela did not direct his followers in an individualist (or brutish, for that matter) tone, but held steadfast to the values and standards that his nation needed to see and hear. The inspiration that this created was famously recognised by a thankful nation and he was rewarded with a Nobel Peace Prize.

What Mandela showed us was that leadership is not just the ability to (directly) guide, but also the aptitude to (indirectly) influence, by upholding the right set of standards and values in a way that resonates with followers on a fundamental level. That means that a leader does not need to deliver speeches that leave a crowd in shock and awe, but just be consistent in the authenticity of their actions.

I can imagine the introverts among us reading that last sentence with great relief. Please rest assured that it is true; my greatest mentor and some of the greatest leaders I have ever met have been of a quiet and retiring nature, but they were also willing to stand up and be counted when the situation called for it.

A modern example began in September 2016 when two professional American football players 'took a knee' during the pre-match national anthem. This was to protest against racial injustice and was met with a 'patriotic' backlash. Both players were quickly vilified and suspended from all future National Football League (NFL) matches.

The actions of those athletes encapsulated the concept of moral responsibility, in this instance by a display of selfless leadership in aid of a greater cause. The NFL deliberated at length and realised their error and then duly lifted the suspensions, but only one player chose to be reinstated. The other (Colin Kaepernick, San Francisco 49ers quarterback) decided to continue to protest in the hope of inspiring meaningful change.

Kaepernick's campaign quickly began to lose traction and it appeared it was doomed for failure, until new life was breathed into the controversy by Nike in 2018. They changed the dynamic by featuring Kaepernick in a 'Just Do It' advertising campaign where his face appeared alongside the slogan 'Believe in something. Even if it means sacrificing everything. Just do it'. Thanks to Nike, and Kaepernick's tenacious attitude, this aspirational moral stance put the argument squarely back in the public domain.

Nike did initially suffer from their bravery, with a 3.9% drop in their share price which was attributed to their support of Kaepernick. The country's President at the time eagerly took to Twitter to display his dismay 'until they stand for the flag'. However, regardless of the President shooting from the hip, the American public began to understand and appreciate the rationale behind 'the knee', and Nike's share price soon recovered (with sales growing by 30%).

Kaepernick had been successful in showing that employment can and almost certainly should be far more than holding a certain amount of technical proficiency that allows someone to 'do a thing'; it plays a significant role in defining a professional as a person. This means that, whether as an individual or an organisation, there certainly appears to be a positive impact on brand and public perception when leadership is combined with unwavering passion that is based upon moral responsibility.

Conversely, the point is also proven by the reputational damage suffered by the NFL because of the dispute. Both Kaepernick and Nike have shown us that a principled stance built on the back of a) what we do and b) what we do it for (purpose) enhances both the amount of professional influence we have, as well as the entire working experience.

The influence of values was also demonstrated within the UK population's paradox of compliance with the COVID-19 restrictions, and the government's efforts to encourage public conformity. The data suggests the pivotal tipping point hinged upon the behaviour of one senior aide to Boris Johnson, Dominic Cummings. When it was found that this person had travelled with his family during lockdown (whilst his wife was reportedly showing COVID symptoms), Cummings was understandably perceived to have undermined the strict public health messaging of the time.

The public's disapproval of this behaviour was not then appeased by the expected apology and resignation of the aide; instead, it was inflamed by him keeping his job and the government shoring its defences and attempting to justify his actions. This 'loophole' thinking critically damaged the nation's collective trust in the government and created a very definite 'them and us' perspective within the public ranks.

Due to this, the nation informally concluded (through the screens of click-bait media and the pages of red tops) that we were not actually 'in this together' after all, and it was every person for themselves.

This inspired a dangerous game of cat and mouse that was not being played out with the virus, but instead with the pandemic rules. At this point, the nation's collective gaze shifted away from the virus, and toward a damaging social injustice regarding the (in)equality in the application of the restrictions.

The disarray that followed reinforces the importance of a leader creating an environment where values preside and all other action falls to conformity as the default. An accompanying culture based on integrity must be 'lived' by all (regardless of position) and reinforced by messages of collective success where positive behaviour is rewarded, and the righting of 'wrongs' is both visible and transparent.

As discussed in the case of Dominic Cummings, the pandemic gave several examples of those hailed as courageous leaders being exposed as little more than loud voices; whilst others with a timid voice stepped up to help us triumph over adversity (Sir Christopher Whitty springs to mind). Let us, then, identify those repeatable leadership traits that were successful:

- **Inspirational vision:** This needs to blend seamlessly with company values and be powerful enough to overcome the expected challenges that lie ahead. This creates a self-supporting collective that aspires to achieve something that resonates with them all.
- **Visible, relevant and accessible:** This means being responsive by prioritising things like one-on-ones (never cancel these), being present during conversations, and always being on time. Nothing devalues someone more than giving them the impression that your time is more important than theirs.

- **Empowerment:** This means personnel have clarity on what is expected, and are confident that they can decide how to achieve those aims in a way that fits their circumstances. The journey doesn't matter so much as the outcome.
- **Authority:** You will naturally influence by being an active listener, seeking to understand and distinguishing between needs and wants, so that you implement changes with a positive impact.
- **Development of personnel:** The employment contract is a management tool; a leader fosters a psychological contract built on mutual trust and respect. Investment in the right personnel will offer the biggest returns.
- **Mutual respect of the work-life balance:** Just because work has crept inside the home, it does not mean previous levels of privacy need to be sacrificed. Work requests are for work hours only; there must be a part of life without work.

When the 'noise' is removed, we should be left with the same values that were shaping our pre-pandemic leadership style(s). The difference is that a remote office shifts the emphasis from saying to doing, which means people are increasingly judged on actions and not perceptions – which, in my opinion, could be seen as a significant step in the right direction.

I would also highlight that the office does not, and should not, provide a mental health silver bullet that is intrinsically linked with a feeling of belonging. This baseless argument was used to encourage people to rush back to offices in the name of well-being. Whilst everyone's circumstances are different, our social interactions are our own choice, not our employer's. Life does not, and should not, revolve around work.

There are many aspects for and against home, office, or hybrid working that range from cost saving (carbon and £) to risk reduction (travel and infection). What is clear, in many cases, is that current management thinking does not match today's workplace reality; however, when it does catch up, then many of us could be swapping 'al-desko dining' for the comfort of our own kitchen.

These types of changes and constant evolutions within the leadership journey can be incredibly rich and engaging, but it is not always a bed of roses. There are pitfalls, most of which can be avoided by being self-aware enough to ensure you don't catch a leadership 'disease'.

Edward 'Richard' Holmes, CBE, TD, JP, VR (1946–2011) was a British Army (reserve) Brigadier and co-director of Cranfield University's Security and Resilience Group. He later became the Professor of Military and Security Studies at the same university and is responsible for much of the contemporary thinking behind leadership as a discipline.

One of the exceptional insights Professor Holmes gave us was the ten diseases of leadership. His belief was that if a leader could recognise these dysfunctional behaviours, then they could also enact self-correcting recovery strategies. With that in mind, here are ten short summaries of the afflictions:

- **Lack of moral courage:** Failing to do the right thing when you know you should.

- **Opposition can be loyal:** Not recognising a subordinate's moral courage to challenge.
- **Consent and evade:** Agreeing with a superior's plan, even though you disagree with it.
- **'You don't need to know':** Reinforce authority by reducing other's ability to contribute.
- **'I've made up my mind':** Driving a plan, regardless of new information or changes.
- **Perfect solutions:** Delay decision-making because of an insatiable need for information.
- **Equating quality with rank:** Not recognising that insight is not inextricably linked to rank.
- **'I am too busy to win':** So blinkered that you fail to identify and exploit opportunities.
- **'I can do your job too':** Retreating into your comfort zones and then micromanaging.
- **Big soldier, cold shadow:** Outwardly successful, but inwardly creating negative climates.

Although all ten diseases are relatively easy to spot in others, self-identification is not so simple. The danger is that the diseases go unnoticed and evolve from short-term intrusions to long-term destructive habits. In short, if things are going wrong in terms of your leadership, then be humble enough to begin the investigation at your own doorstep because you may have caught a leadership disease!

Perhaps an eleventh disease could involve that charismatic bunch known as 'natural' leaders, who tend to exhibit behaviours that serendipitously fall close to those we have previously described. This is only effective to a point and should not be trusted when high levels of leadership are required. In effect, your Sunday league captain may struggle to lead your organisation.

I have seen great leaders in action, and not all had the job title you might expect. I have also seen 'competent' managers, many with impressive job titles, but with no functional competence in leadership (more common than you may think). The following underappreciated processes help bridge the gap between management and leadership:

- **Job Descriptions:** Clearly defined roles and responsibilities result in interdependent bonds and engagement. They must remain agile; nobody wants to hear 'but that's not my job'. However, it is important to recognise that every cog in a wheel needs to function as designed, and that certain tasks are dependent upon specialist skills. Using a responsible, accountable, consulted and informed (RACI) chart works well to coordinate all the activities or decision-making authorities undertaken set against the backdrop of the personnel and their roles.
- **Performance:** Monitoring organisational progress will reveal the degree to which resources are returning on investment. Early identification of anomalies will minimise disruption and enhance a cultural shift from continuous improvement (an effort) to operational excellence (a mindset). Beware, however, as nothing destroys a growth culture like management by numbers.

- **Management system:** Policies and procedures should form the organisational parts into a harmonious collective of synergies. There is NO need for an extensive compendium, only what is necessary to enable an agreed set of principles to achieve objectives by informed decision-making and resource collaboration. An overfocus on any ISO could hold you back.

In terms of all three of the above, the Stevenson/Farmer review 'Thriving at Work' was commissioned in 2017 by the UK's then Prime Minister, Theresa May. It delivered an 'inescapable conclusion that it is massively in the interest both of employers and government to prioritise and invest far more in improving mental health'.

Not only is managing this risk a legal requirement, but is unarguably the right thing to do. With that in mind, the UK regulator used the review to develop a framework of six management system standards with the aim to reduce the negative impact of work on mental health:

- The first standard addresses job **demands** and includes workload, patterns, and environment. This standard enables a workforce to cope with the demands of their jobs, and requires the skills and abilities of a job to be designed with the capabilities of the worker in mind.
- The second standard is about the **control** and influence a person has in the way they conduct work. This standard empowers the worker and gives them, where possible, autonomy over their work (pace, patterns and breaks) whilst encouraging skills development and initiative.

- The third standard is about **support** and includes the sponsorship required to ensure workers have the backing they need from colleagues and management. This requires policies that enact and enable managers to support their staff and peers to crucially support each other.
- The fourth standard concerns **relationships** and results in a workforce that are confident that they work in a safe environment and are not subject to unacceptable behaviours. An organisation must implement necessary systems to prevent, report, and resolve unacceptable behaviour.
- The fifth standard concerns the actual job **role** and ensures an understanding of roles and responsibilities. This results in a workforce that are comfortable and confident in performing their tasks and requires an analysis of the compatibility of the workers and job descriptions.
- The last standard relates to **change** and how it is managed to create an engaged and informed workforce who can then anticipate and raise concerns in good time. This requires timely communication, as well as the opportunity for consultation to influence the process.

In relation to mental health, an article was published in the *Lancet* by the Australian Fire Service, which concluded that a mental health programme aimed at managers has the potential to return £9.98 for each pound spent. We know that poor mental health costs the UK economy £74-£99 billion per year, and those figures do not include the human cost felt by loved ones behind closed doors.

Perhaps the actual debate that we should all be talking about is that, while leadership is always needed, the days of management oversight may be numbered. However, this transition can only take place when we rid ourselves of a couple of workplace pariahs:

- **Presenteeism** generally involves poor work behaviours and an 'eye on the clock' mentality that falls far below the expectations of both peers and management. In the UK, this disappointingly common trait is thought to be practised by 80% of the workforce (2019), with another 25% under the distinctly depressing impression that it is increasing.
- **Leavism** was coined in 2014 by Professor Cary Cooper of Manchester University and describes the practice of using flexitime and/or other leave entitlement to conduct work during non-paid hours. Research in 2018 by the Chartered Institute of Personnel and Development revealed that 72% of respondents had observed leavism, with another 37% admitting guilt.

What is equally concerning is that there is an increasing amount of evidence that those employees who are constantly digitally available are being overly favoured by employers. This means that the remote world is now taking large strides to mirror the physical world in terms of presenteeism (proximity bias).

The eradication of presenteeism and leavism is now an important task within the role of any competent management function. It is vital that we are cognisant of these types of unhealthy behaviours and uncomfortable truths. What is certain is that a manager of any level cannot, in good faith, talk about motivation and performance without facilitating a workspace where employees feel trusted to conduct their function, without fear of a real or perceived penalty.

In conclusion, leadership is a discipline based on principles and practised by professionals who develop a range of styles, each of which are engineered and then polished to elicit a required outcome. The best leaders lead from the heart and build respect by enacting a set of meaningful values that resonate with their subordinates on a fundamental level. The great managers complement leadership by creating a consistent and fair environment for success. If you can successfully combine the two, then you will have mastered an art (leadership) and conquered a science (management).

Chapter Two

Motivation, Engagement & Building Teams

'Alone, we can do so little; together, we can do so much.'

–Helen Keller

I remember sitting in a lecture theatre during my first undergraduate semester at Edinburgh University and learning about Professor George Elton Mayo (1880–1949). The one story that sticks in my mind was set at Western Electric's Hawthorne plant (Chicago) and took place in 1924.

The facility in question made telephones and had a reputation for innovative management techniques, so they welcomed a study from a prominent scientist into the relationship between lighting and workforce efficiency. As soon as the study began, the researchers noticed a correlation.

However, what they did not expect to discover was that efficiency increased regardless of the change that was made to the lighting. This resulted in the initial hypothesis being that output was stimulated by light change, and not light level.

The researchers then introduced other changes and found that any change increased worker output. Their first thought was that the increases must be the result of the frequent rest breaks between experiments. The thinking was that the breaks led to more social interactions, which had a positive impact on workforce attitudes and, hence, efficiency (even 100 years ago, we knew that a 'happy' workforce was a productive workforce).

The friendly supervisory style that was adopted during the study was also noted, as well as the fact that it had created a certain esprit de corps. However, Mayo did not buy into that, and his view was that the workers were enjoying the attention, and so had engaged with the project (and workplace) on a higher level.

To prove his hypothesis, he initiated a series of interviews and, to everyone's surprise except his own, found that the most powerful catalyst for output was a sense of belonging that was fostered because of the increased dialogue between the workers and their employer.

In effect, Mayo had shown that humans are social animals, and the key to their performance was not to rearrange machinery, shout or offer money, but to listen and talk. By adopting a conversational and compassionate approach, Mayo had linked the style of supervision with morale, which he was then able to show had a bearing on productivity.

Mayo also found that the workers developed their own code of behaviour, which was enhanced in solidarity when they were challenged by external elements (such as the employer). It was also discovered that it was the workers who dictated work rate, and not the management. In a collaborative team environment, informal hierarchy trumps formal hierarchy every time. This clearly shows that legacy managers rarely have, or have ever had, the amount of control and influence that they believe.

In short, we have Mayo to thank for proving that job satisfaction drives productivity, and that both were far more reliant on social belonging than any transactional incentives and/or working conditions.

It was also Mayo who highlighted the need for a more humanistic approach to industrial behaviour and human relations. However, over 100 years later, expensive management consultants still point us towards technical solutions when addressing workplace performance challenges. This is counter-intuitive when the history books tell us that quicker, cheaper, and more effective solutions come from simply asking what motivates a worker (Mayo provides a case in point to that effect).

This brings us neatly on to motivational psychology, which can be thought of as the study of cognitive processes that create mental states that drive us forward. This is the unseen force that powers workers through difficult journeys and great hardships that often do not seem commensurate to their hourly wage. Part of a manager's job is to be able to access that engine to ensure workers consistently fulfil their job function, and go that extra mile when needs be.

In day-to-day practice, a manager has many motivational theories that they can choose from to inspire their workforce. Having an awareness of most of them is an advantage, whilst having a working knowledge of at least a few is essential. To cover that point, here is an overview of the most common theories currently in practice:

Competence theory is based on the concept that individuals want to engage in employment to showcase their skills. This hinges on the value the individual places on praise and means the person must engage in challenging tasks linked to psychologically safe feedback loops.

Expectancy theory assumes that workers are selfish by nature, and bases behaviours on what they believe leads to the most desirable outcome for them. This environment is created by setting challenging but achievable goals which are duly incentivised with attractive rewards.

Incentive theory suggests that reinforcement and recognition generate motivation, and different rewards inspire different behaviours (sustainable versus short term). This means certain goals are better paired with different rewards: bonus, development, promotion, salary, time off, etc.

McClelland's need theory tells us that each person is driven by three needs, regardless of age, gender, or culture: affiliation involving meaningful connections; a desire to achieve; and power to influence.

I have left **Maslow's hierarchy of needs** for last, as it is arguably the most common and successful workplace motivation theory. It involves satisfying five levels of workforce need:

- **Physical** is the lowest level and includes the fundamentals needed for survival. This would involve paying a fair salary so that workers can obtain what they perceive as necessities.
- **Safety** is the need for a sense of protection. This spans a range in the workplace from feeling physically safe to also being comfortable in terms of having job security.
- **Socialisation** is the human tendency to 'belong'. In a workplace, meeting outside of a professional setting fosters connections with colleagues (lunches, team building, etc.).
- **Esteem** involves status and using recognition (see Expectancy Theory). This requires a workplace mechanism that recognises achievements by providing positive feedback.
- **Self-actualisation** is a growth-orientated state that is achieved by satisfying all the other four levels (physical, safety, socialisation, and esteem).

Workplace motivation should never be thought of as a point-in-time project. It is an ongoing aspirational journey that can never be truly fulfilled (the human condition dictates that certain perfections can never be achieved). This means that, regardless of the chosen theory (or mix, thereof), it is critical to the organisational culture that you keep abreast of progress being made through focus groups, consultation, climate surveys, etc. It is very easy for this aspect to turn into a toxic element.

So, if you haven't thought about which motivation theory is right for your company, then it is time to start. Not only has this been shown to be a golden ticket to increase profit and productivity, but it creates a happier workforce whose engagement makes them far less inclined to look for other employment.

Interestingly, there is not a universally accepted definition of engagement, but the phrase 'emotional connection' is often used. However, the discretionary commitment and connection to an organisation's goals and values is generally accepted. In essence, when an employee feels engaged, they are invested in organisational success.

This kind of positive stasis causes the workforce to produce their best work, whilst ensuring their positive influence extends to the wider collective group by offering further benefits. A meta-analysis in 2016, involving 339 research studies across 230 businesses, proved this by exploring the relationship between performance and employee engagement. It concluded that top- and bottom-quartile variations were in the region of: 21% in profitability; 20% in sales; 70% in safety incidents; and 41% in absenteeism.

It is within these critical business areas that an effective employee engagement strategy can offer a huge multiplier on the return on investment. It would be a common mistake to think that the focus of such an initiative is to make everyone happy with a journey that involves defining employee satisfaction (in terms of needs and wants) and matching those criteria within the organisation's vision and mission. This is especially salient in today's world when employees are searching for a perfect employer.

This type of aspirational search has spawned a 'war for talent' and prompted two thirds of companies to cite employee retention as a greater concern than initially finding the right candidate. This is reflected in the research, with three quarters of employees in 2022 saying they are open to offers, of which over a fifth would not even need an increase of pay, and almost three quarters of which would accept a reduction in money. This demonstrates to us that contemporary metrics have evolved beyond cash, and now lean far more towards the remit of 'engagement'.

We cannot ignore that most teachings on this subject are based on a flawed assumption that the workforce is rational and engaged. A meta-analysis in 2017 revealed that only 29% (on average) of a workforce will be engaged, with the remaining 71% on a steep sliding scale of disengagement. MBA-required readings and TED Talks tend to forget to mention the latter portion of the workforce where your trust will not always be respected, what you give is not always what you get in return, and empathy would most likely be viewed as an exploitable vulnerability.

I have seen many other potential traps over the years during my time witnessing, authoring, and assessing employee engagement strategies. One of the most common issues that hamper engagement strategies is the tendency of the management function to adopt a financially driven transactional approach. This is because managers like things that can be measured, because that type of outcome makes for a better presentation when it comes to justifying headcount and budgets to a senior leadership team.

However, despite the overwhelming evidence indicating that engagement cannot be bought, and the transactional approach is pointless, organisations continue to employ golden handcuffs in a fruitless attempt to retain talent. Although research does reveal that enhanced pay yields short-term benefit, it has been shown to have little meaningful effect on medium-term retention or performance.

What have been found to be far more effective tools in relation to retention and performance are behavioural traits (such as trust) that lead to relationship enablers. Studies show that high-trust companies report up to 50% higher productivity, 13% fewer sick days, and 40% less burnout.

Neuroscience has found that such trust is founded upon the release of a chemical called oxytocin. Interestingly, we can stimulate the release of oxytocin within our workforce, and the following are five simple (and proven) examples of how managers can build on this:

- Oxytocin activates when we **build social connections** because nobody wants to let their team down. So, progressive managers tend to think beyond task-only driven scheduling.
- Workplaces benefit from **helping employees develop personally**, with investment in the person creating engagement. This includes work-life balance, recreation, reflection, etc.
- **Peer-to-peer recognition** using the power of the crowd to celebrate successes has been shown to inspire others to aim for excellence and gives top talent a forum for them to share.
- Assigning **achievable challenges** releases oxytocin and adrenocorticotropic hormone (ACTH) to intensify focus and

strengthen connections, so that teams can work together more effectively.

- Once deemed competent, allowing employees to manage and execute in their own way (**autonomy**) promotes innovation. Quite simply, different people try different things.

As Richard Branson puts it, 'A business has to be involving, it has to be fun, and it has to exercise your creative instincts.' What we can be confident of is that high performers need collaborative environments where they are free to express themselves, make decisions (without micromanagement), and the entrepreneurship that separates them from 'the pack' is recognised, encouraged, and rewarded.

It is a rite of passage for a senior manager to realise that it is their people, especially the high performers, that dictate their individual and collective success as a leader. This is especially important in a tight labour market where competition for top talent is plentiful. So, put down the spreadsheet and ask yourself what you need to do to build trust if you want to build great teams.

Several studies show that diverse groups of 'normal' people consistently outperform homogenous teams of objectively high-ability problem solvers. This tells us that we do not need a team of 'stars', especially in the complex analysis and scientific research fields, but that team does need a degree of diversity.

By their very nature, diversity includes the challenges that are brought about by our differences. Humans are inherently tribal and, if the fear of 'others' gains traction, then it becomes a toxic performance inhibitor.

This means it is critical for success to mitigate that potential friction. One of the best ways to bridge that gap is by uniting the team behind a common purpose that supersedes any other perceived issues, which means building on a self-supporting collective purpose and rallying behind a shared vision.

So, if you want a group that quickly and easily arrives at a collective consensus, then you must ensure it does not contain outliers. But, if you are willing to create a group from a spectrum of 'types', you will be repaid with a deeper pool of solutions that will offer smarter outcomes. This means that a great team does not need the best and the brightest; instead, it requires diverse thinking styles and a leader that can engage the collective in a vision that means more than their differences.

Patrick Lencioni, the *New York Times* best-selling author who published *The Five Dysfunctions of a Team* (2002), knows this. He gave us the Lencioni Trust Pyramid and, as with Maslow's pyramid, this underappreciated gem works to explain development, dynamics, and teambuilding. The Lencioni Trust Pyramid is divided into five layers and follows the principle of foundation before elevation.

With that in mind, it builds from the bottom up, meaning the previous layer must be satisfied to effectively pass onto the next:

- **Layer one (trust versus invulnerability):** establishing standards and values is the start of it all. This allows open dialogue to challenge, voice concerns and admit errors. If workload or team ability are mentioned in hushed tones at the coffee machine, then there is still work to do.

- **Layer two (constructive conflicts versus artificial harmony):** constructive conflicts, not confrontation, lead to vivid and active engagement that results in progress. This is an intrinsic part of a functioning team to ensure it does not operate within a false economy of mediocrity.
- **Layer three (involvement versus vagueness):** involvement can only be high when the previous levels are satisfied; and, although there may be solidarity, unity requires that choices be taken without doubting, and this can only happen once arguments from both sides are heard.
- **Layer four (responsibility versus low standard):** although this is often thought of as an individual characteristic, the team also has a responsibility for behaviours, attitudes, and results. Ignoring this responsibility results in differing views about the quality of results.
- **Layer five (results versus status/ego):** a major frustration can be the tendency to be distracted by aspects other than the objectives. A focused team minimises individualistic behaviours which jeopardise collective success; and, in general, a successful team is a happy team.

It is clear to see that working as a cohesive collective adds immeasurable benefits. However, as with all relationships (hard to not draw a comparison with marriage), this needs constant work to foster the intended outcome, and this is a leader's defining responsibility. This ethos has been encapsulated by Brentford Football Club in their 2021/22 season. The West London club gained promotion to the

Premier League for the first time since 1947, and it makes me ask what can we learn from their unstoppable team momentum.

The secret to that success appears to be a recruitment and transfer strategy based on logic, data, and statistical analytics. Club owner Matthew Benham, a former Oxford graduate, had done something similar with Danish side FC Midtjylland in 2014. That club won the Danish Superliga 2014-15, 2017-18, 2019-20, and were runners-up in 2018-19 and 2020-21. Prior to Benham's influence, the best that FC Midtjylland had achieved were runners-up in 2007-08.

The philosophy that Benham uses is to look at potential, and not actual, performance. This means searching for players that do the right things, but do not necessarily deliver the right outcomes. For example:

- Attacking players are not judged by goals, but considered in terms of runs, dribbles, and passes.
- Defenders are not looked at by clean sheets, but on chances they provide opposition attackers.
- Goalkeepers are examined by shot stopping and areas where they concede (an aspect that can be controlled by a defensive line).

There is also an interesting profile in terms of age range. The club's investment in younger players of a lower value has resulted in the average age of signing being below 23; only four of the regular starters are over 27 years old, with a single player over the age of 30. This approach brings several benefits, one of which facilitates an attacking style that forces the older players to perform.

This has caused Brentford to look in places that other such clubs do not, like the second division in France or lower divisions in Denmark. The returns on this strategy are impressive, with several examples of players that cost a million euros each being valued at 12 and 10.5 million euros, respectively.

By diversifying away from ticket reliance and into the transfer market, the club was also able to weather the pandemic far better than most. Brentford's revenue for the year end of the 2020 season was £13.9 million and, at the time of writing, the club is now chasing a minimum of £297 million over the next five years (if the team survives the Premiership season). This means that a club that many had not heard of only 15 years ago is now competing for one of the biggest prizes in sport.

What Benham can teach us about building teams is to:

- Look beyond the immediate professional and explore the potential of the individual.
- Pay less attention to specific pedigree, and more towards a varied multi-discipline background.
- Look beyond the 'usual' universities to lesser academic institutions and vocational avenues.
- Look to develop an employee internally, rather than hiring a more 'finished' product.

Finally, he will tell us that if we want to successfully disrupt and change for the better, then we must stop doing what we've always done and step outside the status quo. Creating such a collective synergy is an aspirational ‘good-to-great’ process that could never be termed a science; but it could be referred to as an abstract art by those fortunate enough to have witnessed it in action.

As with any art form, and discounting sheer luck, the mechanisms must conform to fundamental rules that are applied at the mercy of the artist. One such principle relates to a dichotomy between transactional versus relational influences that is generally underestimated or miscalculated by the management function.

Transactional teams are number-driven cultures characterised by financial metrics. These paid-per-unit ‘piece-rate’ models are generally populated by those who thrive on being ahead of the pack, at the ‘top of their game’, and who require a leader who appreciates their longevity, within the close context of burnout ratios. These teams are exceptionally successful within certain remits, but must be closely monitored as the lure of the prize can frequently supersede personal and/or corporate integrity (case in point: Enron).

Relational teams sit at the other end of the spectrum within a far more complex social construct, where the psychological contract is elevated far beyond the documented employment equivalent. The metrics used to measure success propel interaction by demonstrating integral values which encompass a strong collective purpose. These types of teams need to be closely monitored to ensure that their competitive viability is not unduly sacrificed by an aggregated comfort zone.

The difference between these types of teams can be clearly seen during times of boom and bust, where their popularity oscillates between financial gain (transactional dominance) and career security (relational growth). This correlation is also apparent on a granular level, where individuals tend to choose contractor-type roles during positive market conditions, but will fall back into full-time employment when times are perceived as uncertain.

One of the most interesting aspects within this paradox is the realisation that no individual or team will ever consistently adopt one principle. There may be times when the inclination is towards one, but a hybrid model will organically dominate to reveal a cultural-shaping dynamic that reflects the combined nature of the team members. This is valuable information in terms of motivation techniques.

It is common to select team members on individual and collective competencies. I would offer that, in order to select a 'great' team, we look beyond competency considerations and reverse engineer our desired culture to the required personality types, which will give a hybrid model that yields a winning culture.

Therefore, both sport and business are full of examples of a team of 'good' consistently outperforming a collection of 'great'. We should not forget that the most successful teams are not necessarily filled with the best players; rather, they are a home for a diverse set of the best team members.

For example, age diversity is one such factor that has proven value and relates to the four very distinct generations that make up our workforce. Each of these groups require tailored leadership and management approaches, and none appear to collectively appreciate each other without a certain amount of assistance in bridging their nuances:

Baby Boomers (born: 1945-1964) were raised in post-war affluence funded by government subsidies and are inextricably linked with consumerism. They worked hard and saw increasing standards of living, the cost of which was decreasing parental supervision (hence 'latchkey' children).

Generation X (born: 1965-1981) inherited an individualistic approach to work that was, and continues to be, characterised by focus, ambition, and an overriding sense of duty to get the job done no matter what the personal cost.

Generation Y/Millennials (born: 1982-1994) had to embrace a worldwide economic crisis where workplace values evaporated; a fact that was lost on bewildered Baby Boomers and Generation X, who ambushed the Millennials for their lack of emotional and social etiquette (using adjectives such as 'entitled').

Lastly, **Generation S (born: 1995-2010)** were endearingly dubbed the 'Centennials'. These are the constantly 'connected' children, youth, and young adults who live in an information age of immediate satisfaction, where the journey has been forgotten in place of a quick-hit of end-result dopamine.

In this world, there is a growing need for us all to be multi-generational in our appreciation of others, no matter how much we are personally anchored within our own attitudes. This is just one reminder that we are not all the same and do not all share the same ideals surrounding self-actualisation. This is because we are unique in our culture, personality, gender, history, sexuality, ability, and attitude – and that everything that makes us unique should be celebrated.

I am sure that it won't surprise you, but I believe in an inclusive workspace where all team members feel appreciated, valued, welcomed, integrated, and included in an accepted space that rewards effort and celebrates the value within our individual diversity.

The point is that the fifth-dimensional space in our ever-changing industry could be an incredibly interesting generational gap that is seemingly ignored within most contemporary management and leadership theories. Performance of and care for our people could be enhanced by framing those essential criteria with consideration for our diverse audience.

One such relatively low-level (but very effective and strangely interesting) strategy that encourages engagement can be seen within the House of Lords' dining room, a place which is the centre point for British eccentricity. This custom does not permit any table reservations and so obliges the peers to sit in the next available seat.

This convention helps to develop a productive camaraderie within the group of multi-party affiliated members. The Lords make this custom work due to their appreciation of collaboration in their lifelong appointment within the upper house, as opposed to the 'revolving door' of the Commons where individuals get voted in and voted out in relatively short durations.

However, in such an inclusive space, we must also be careful to ensure that groups do not necessarily lose their identity and then blend and disappear into the collective 'trend'. In this context, let's think of groups as project teams or departments. The idea is not that the sentiment of each group is lost to make the larger 'one team', but that the groups' separate points and perspectives are respected and considered within the overall strategy by a leadership team that recognises them.

I remember reading an interview transcript between McKinsey and rugby All Black legend Bill Osbourne, which was an enjoyable and insightful piece in terms of trust and respect. For context, Bill Osbourne was the outgoing president of New Zealand Rugby and a celebrated player in his own right. He wore the black jersey an impressive 48 times from 1975 to 1982 (including 16 international tests).

He is also one of the rare breed who was able to translate his rugby success into the business world. This resulted in him holding senior roles at the New Zealand Post and Quotable Value New Zealand, as well as sitting on several corporate and charitable boards. This means we can say with confidence, in terms of business and rugby, that he knows what he is talking about.

Considering Osbourne's significant amount of success, I really admire his humbleness. When asked what permeated most from his time with the All Blacks into his post-rugby career, his answer was the adoption of the Māori beliefs: whakapapa and kaitiakitanga.

Whakapapa is the understanding of the 'genealogical descent of all living things from God to the present time... in the respect of the creation and development of all things'. This is more than mere lineage (far deeper than blood); it is best described as a spiritual appreciation of the way the universe has conspired to create a person and their place within it. A fascinating concept.

Kaitiakitanga is a code of conduct (deeply rooted in ethical values) and a Māori kaitiaki is a keeper, preserver, and conservator. It can be thought of as the concept of guardianship and protection of whakapapa (the very essence of the Māori people). This involves a connection between the spiritual, human, and natural world and can apply to a group or an individual.

Considering the philosophical gravity of these concepts, it is clear why the All Blacks take to the pitch with a distinctive mindset. Rugby coaches all over the world eagerly tell players to 'play for the badge'; however, pulling on the black jersey means that, for the next 80 minutes, you are a custodian, not just of the shirt and the badge, but the ancestral path of all Māori. Now, that makes for a strong team ethos.

An example of more complex team dynamics, specifically in terms of motivation, engagement, and team building, could be seen within the Battle of Mosul. This was the most comprehensive military operation since the Iraq War in 2003, and the toughest urban conflict since World War II (WWII). It began on 16 October 2016 and involved up to 12,000 fighters from the Islamic State of Iraq and al-Sham (ISIS) who faced a patchwork of Iraqi and coalition forces that numbered over 100,000.

In 2014, ISIS forces took Mosul in only five days and added it to their growing stock of over 100,000 square kilometres of Iraq. ISIS duly fortified the city and turned it into their regional headquarters. Between 2014 and 2016, Iraqi forces worked with coalition forces to go on the offensive and reclaimed Tikrit (April 2015), Ramadi (March 2016) and Fallujah (June 2016).

The attacking force for Mosul was commanded by Lieutenant General Abdul Amir Yarallah. The plan was to surround the city and then split it in half by destroying the five Tigris bridges from the air. Following this, forces would take eastern then western Mosul. The exhaustion of the different forces was to be prevented by using 'bite, clear, and hold' tactics. This meant that seasoned units would take an area before handing it to a lesser unit and recuperating. The offensive was to take three months.

Operations began in October 2016 and 30% of the city was taken in the first month. All bridges were destroyed in December, and in January Prime Minister Haider al-Abadi announced the liberation of eastern Mosul. The next push came in February 2017, which involved control of the Old City and the al-Nuri Mosque and caused horrendous casualties on both sides. Then, on 9 July 2017 (after nine months), Prime Minister al-Abadi declared Mosul fully liberated.

Points of interest:

- **Military importance ≠ value:** ISIS left the coalition no option but to act with decisive force when ISIS declared Mosul the caliphate and principal economic hub.

- **Civilians add untold complexity:** A minority will not and sometimes cannot leave.
- **Attackers prevail at a big cost:** Mosul demonstrated this axiom with ISIS using concealment, fortified buildings, subterranean systems, etc.
- **Agile attacker-to-defender ratios:** This conflict had a far higher ratio than the 3-to-1 standard due, in part, to the coalition not being unified.
- **Supply chain appreciation:** Urban warfare has a 360-degree reality and uses up to four times the amount of ammunition than a rural environment.
- **New technology adds advantage:** Weaponised UAVs were used by both sides to great effect as surveillance, reconnaissance, and direct fire platforms.
- **Armour works:** The myth that armour does not suit urban settings was proven wrong again (Mosul, Mogadishu, Belfast, etc.).
- **Synergy analysis:** ISIS used UAVs to guide in vehicle IEDs containing 482 suicide bombers.

The Battle of Mosul reinforces several of the processes also seen in the Battle of Mogadishu (see Chapter Five), that we can then turn into commercial axioms of our own, such as:

- Pre- and ongoing analysis providing relevant understanding of market, commercial and operational environments is essential in engagement.

- The above point must be combined with a unified approach of a multi-disciplinary technologically enabled team that independently and interdependently appreciates its role in creating collective value within deliverables.

In conclusion to this chapter, Professor George Elton Mayo has shown us that shouting and money mean very little, and that relationships and engagement win games. This is especially true if we take the time to carefully build and motivate a team of individuals with the right traits who can flourish in an environment of trust and respect. However, we cannot forget that the 71% will bring us challenges; but this thought must be leveraged against the fact that inclusive, diverse, and technologically enabled teams get the best results.

Chapter Three

Strategy, Governance & Business Systems

'Always start at the end before you begin.'

–Robert Kiyosaki

ESG refers to the environmental, social and governance impact of an organisation's activity, and is one of the most important and misunderstood terms in the business world. The acronym originates from the money markets, where investors would assign individual 'E', 'S' and 'G' criteria to help see beyond the potential financial outcomes of their investment and understand the wider impact that their financing may have on global issues. The cynical among us can rest assured that there is also strong evidence that ESG-led investments hold less risk (so it is effectively a moral and economic win/win).

If we look at the impact of ESG on the workings of a business, then we can begin to appreciate why it yields a more favourable risk profile. In terms of ESG influence on internal processes, 'social' and 'governance' are the most relevant. This would include workforce interface (social), as well as decision-making and leadership (governance). This encapsulates diversity and inclusion, talent attraction and retention, engagement, health and well-being, etc. It is easy to see why those with high ESG scores (from organisations who are progressive by nature) have far more favourable and stable margins.

Conversely, beyond the internal inefficiencies of those firms without an ESG-focus, negative publicity and reputational damage is a key investment risk. For example, P&O Ferries were vilified in the UK in 2022 when they terminated the employment of 800 workers; and Boohoo was crippled by the accusation of modern slavery due to allegations that they paid workers only £3.50 per hour. Now, imagine the challenge facing multinationals with global supply chains operating in developing countries, where the risk of human trafficking and forced labour is always very real.

This means that ESG is so much more than just the environmental considerations it is generally perceived to be. Of course, now more than ever, the environment should be at the forefront of our decision-making, but we must appreciate there are also many other ways to damage our planet. ESG is your social licence to operate, and far more than just a moral imperative; it is how you make informed decisions about sustainability and ethical impact whilst driving value creation, top-line growth and bottom-line profit.

The stark reality is that the world has matured from when Lisa Minnelli told us that 'money makes the world go round'. Now, your market, clients and workforce demand you 'do the right thing', regardless of cost. However, it is far more than just ESG that drives high-level corporate decisions and strategy.

To examine this wider concept, let's start with the common premise that there are two levels of strategy: business and corporate. The former is concerned with competitive advantage in the relevant market(s), whilst the latter focuses on managing the existing portfolio of businesses in the company.

Although the dual-level strategy might sound simple, it is common for organisations to fail in adding any discernible value to the process by forgetting (or purposely foregoing) the creation of a strategy plan. Omitting this critical phase is akin to going to war on a whim and, to be blunt, that rarely ends well for those on the initiative.

A good strategy plan usually begins by assessing the company's existing businesses, as well as the value added by the wider corporation. This analysis creates the building blocks of the corporate strategy which will ultimately shape and drive the organisation's future actions.

The process generally starts by identifying the opportunities to share activities within the existing business units. This will not only reveal the core business(es) with the potential for competitive advantage, but will also build meaningful interrelationships that could avoid the need for restructure. The opportunity to optimise mutually beneficial interrelationships with other internal businesses is beneficial for almost all (except those not in a core business unit).

Once this has been done, then it gives the option of disposing of non-core businesses. This may involve simply closing them down or waiting for the right buyer. Whichever tactic is followed, the result will free up precious resources to reinvest in the core activities.

After the initial streamlining is complete (which is then ongoing), the focus turns to synergy and optimisation by cross-collaboration, grouping units together and modifying incentives. This will include shared activities on distribution networks, offices, equipment, etc.

If the possibility of shared opportunities is limited, then the company can pursue those that share human capital/competency. However, relying on transferable skills alone is not efficient and is fraught with challenge and uncertainty, and so should be avoided within most markets.

Lastly, the examination of the management function cannot be underestimated. Nearly every industry is littered with undermanaged companies that hold huge untapped potential that can be released by employing a very simple programme of examination and restructuring.

Once these steps are completed, then the company can move to implementation. Some advice: plan and leave the ego at the door – we all know what happened to Gordon Gekko (and, if we do not, then I am delighted this book has reached such a diverse age group!).

However, there are pitfalls to these strategies (especially of not being agile and sticking to them in a blinkered fashion), the video-rental market being a prime example. A highlight of my teenage Friday nights was to visit the local Blockbuster with my father to rent the latest VHS video. At that time, the $3 billion franchise had 84,000 workers and 65 million customers, yet 20 years later it no longer existed.

The first Blockbuster store was opened by David Cook in Dallas on 19 October 1985. Cook was a software developer who had been asked by a friend to investigate the video-rental business. The staff had to lock the doors on that first day to stop overcrowding.

What gave Cook and Blockbuster the competitive edge was a barcode system that could manage up to 10,000 video tapes per store, as opposed to the 100 per store offered by their competitors. It was reputed that they earned $800 million per year through late fees alone!

Cook soon enhanced the operation by building a $6 million distribution centre. This was used to hold a huge number of titles and allowed each store to tailor a range to their local customers. Furthermore, the hub also cut a significant amount of time out of the process required to open a new store.

Cook departed the business after only two years due to irreconcilable disagreements with investors. Wayne Huisenga then took control and embarked on an aggressive expansion plan that involved opening one new store every single day. By 1988, there were over 400 stores!

Although Huisenga saw the value in diversification (mostly through music and video-game rental), he was nervous about emerging technology, particularly cable television. In 1994, Huisenga sold the Blockbuster video-rental business to Viacom for a whopping $8 billion.

In the following two years, Blockbuster stubbornly continued to focus on physical locations, and their value halved. In 1997, Reed Hastings founded a DVD-by-mail company called Netflix, a company that Blockbuster passed on the opportunity to buy for a mere $50 million.

In 2009, Netflix posted $116 million profits, had 3 million customers, and were preparing to launch a streaming service. In the same year, Blockbuster posted $518 million losses and then, on 1 July 2010, was delisted (NYSE) and rented their last video on 9 November 2013.

In this case, a company that was started by a software developer denied the digital age, and their lack of innovation cost them dearly. There are lots of relatable contexts in today's world, from the pandemic to the climate crisis: when facing those challenges, you can be Blockbuster, or you can be Netflix. I guess it all depends on the science around choice and change.

Considering recent years, we all know that there are times when change is the only constant. If that change is well planned and professionally executed, then it can result in positive gains and a healthy journey for those involved, with the opposite also being dangerously true.

The difference between the outcomes can often be the influence of a layer of leadership that is able to competently lead a workforce from point A to point B. It is this group that evokes workforce motivation via consistent delivery of inclusive support and clear direction.

This is not an easy task and is nearly always complicated by a human propensity to undergo an emotional journey involving a degree of resistance and suspicion toward any change. It is in this space that leaders can benefit from anchoring their efforts to a framework for change.

One such framework is the Kubler-Ross Model, commonly referred to as 'the five stages of grief'. What is not so commonly known is that the model can also segment stages of change into digestible chunks. A leader can then use this view to anticipate their personnel's emotional journey, and so gauge the thoughts and feelings of their workforce. For example:

- **Stage One (Denial):** Workforce shock. Whilst being careful not to overwhelm, the leader needs to help personnel understand why the change is happening and how it will be enacted.
- **Stage Two (Anger):** When reality lands, fear of the unknown can manifest itself in anger. At this time, unwavering support, and a commitment to the end goal from the leader, is required.
- **Stage Three (Bargaining):** When change is understood, people try to find the best fit for them. This requires active listening, dialogue, and meaningful consultation from the leader.
- **Stage Four (Depression):** There's no way out, I'm trapped. This brings low energies and a dip in morale. It is important for the leader to empathise whilst energising the future vision.
- **Stage Five (Acceptance):** The change is embraced as the workforce begins to build hopes and aspirations, whilst others have simply resigned themselves to the inevitability of the change.

It goes without saying that the applicability of the five stages is different for everyone, and it is neither linear nor time bound (and so the leadership styles and management techniques must be equally as agile). Also, whilst the Kubler-Ross Model is my preferred option, the

ADKAR model, and John Kotter's eight steps (along with several others) are also excellent in guiding personnel through change.

So, regardless of the type and format you opt for, it is important that a framework is adopted. This is so that you equip your leaders with the skills they need to understand their personnel's emotional journey. Without such knowledge, we cannot be confident of fulfilling our moral, legal, and economic duty to control the negative impacts associated with change.

A related philosophical subject would be that of choice. This is a concept dependent upon the depth of understanding that a decision-maker has about potential outcomes, and the importance they assign to each consequential scenario. A reoccurring strategic error involves the under-estimation of an outcome probability due to an under-appreciation of escalation potential.

You will probably know the process that enables these types of 'unexpected' events to become a reality as the 'law of unintended consequence' – or, as Adam Smith referred to it, 'the invisible hand' (arguably the most famous metaphor in any of the social sciences).

The most prolific example emerged just after World War I with the advent of the Treaty of Versailles. The treaty was to ensure that the German war machine was effectively nullified; in reality, however, it facilitated public support for Hitler, who gained momentum leading up to WWII.

A recent example is that of pandemic mandates, vaccine passports and other restrictions based on vaccination status. Such policies, necessary at the time, also promoted stigma, social polarisation and created a loss of trust in government and public health measures.

What this example teaches is that, for an organisation to be considered 'healthy', it would do well to combine empowerment strategies based on consultation with improving infrastructure to achieve sustainable governance.

Organisational health can be thought of as the equilibrium of three forces: the value of a strategy, measuring how that strategy is translated into action (rhetoric versus reality), and how well the entity evolves to a) keep pace with the external market and b) adapt the internal engine to achieve performance aspirations. A strategy based on developing a cohesive aggregate of those aspects has been shown to deliver up to 50% performance variations and three-fold returns to shareholders.

There is not a 'one size fits all' solution, but evidence does uniformly suggest that the difference between surviving and thriving ('health') is an ability to align, execute, and renew faster than the competition. As the saying goes, those that do not find time for health will need to make time for illness.

These lessons, along with many others, were put into practice by Al-Qaeda when they used terror to seize jihadi primacy on 11 September 2001, causing 2,996 immediate fatalities and 6,000 injured. The subsequent actions by the West against the militant Sunni Islamists group came in the form of Operation Enduring Freedom.

The predictability of the response was repackaged by Al-Qaeda as a Christian-Jewish alliance that conspired to destroy Islam. This PR 'ambush' neutered military dominance and effectively transformed the West's quest for 'liberation' into a perceived revenge campaign. This caused a wave of Islamophobia, which then ignited disenfranchised home-grown warriors within the bedrooms and mosques of the world. In short, anyone who adopts a strategy without taking advice from a competent communications team in riding into war unprepared.

Other strategic lessons that can be taken would be as follows (but is not exhaustive):

- **Empowerment:** Al-Qaeda initially suffered heavy losses, which is why the group offered little resistance to the emergence of the limelight-hungry Islamic State. This redirected the eyes of the West and gave the Al-Qaeda leadership breathing space to reform and decentralise back into the traditional cell framework. This strategy empowered regional satellite groups to re-establish internal regional-specific stability and grow localised strength.
- **Agility:** The result was that the West was then faced with an enemy who used silo growth. To combat this, the West had to spread its military resources dangerously thin to track cells, which generally proved fruitless as they gave up little information relating to the global network. This caused many countries and cultures to leave offensive strategy to the Americans, whilst they fell back on a budget-friendly programme of border control and defence. Quite simply, the Al-Qaeda leadership had prevented the coalition from taking a collaborative initiative.

- **Embrace change:** Due to decentralisation, several splinter groups with aspirations beyond Al-Qaeda formed. One group was a Salafist jihadist organisation known as the Al-Nusra Front (2012) that considered an Islamic alliance to be weak. To address this, the group took six to eight months to transform from the Al-Nusra Front to Hayat Tahrir al-Sham and emerged from that process in 2017 markedly different.
- **Vision:** Due to the dichotomy between the founding and 'new' members, the group quickly fractured, and Tansim Huras al-Din (Guardians of Religion Organisation) was born in late 2017. This group returned to Al-Qaeda loyalty by means of a leader rumoured to have a place within the 12-strong global shura-council. The 'full circle' story is not unique, the Al-Qaeda vision calls their soldier's home.
- **Strategic alliances:** Groups such as Al-Qaeda generally falter when they forge credible partnerships outside of their primary market. Such efforts generally require third-party enforcers and are usually built upon the foundation of mutual destruction if one party betrays the other. However, Al-Qaeda have always had a talent for building relationships (Hezbollah, Chechen rebels, Taliban, etc.).
- **Bridging boundaries:** Some groups that have bridged cultural and geographical boundaries include: Al-Qaeda Islamic Maghreb (AQIM), an Algerian group that moved into Sahel and West Africa; Al-Qaeda Arabian Peninsula (AQAP), formed in a merger of the international Islamic militant network in Yemen

and Saudi Arabia; and Al-Qaeda Indian Subcontinent (AQIS), operating in Afghanistan, Pakistan, India, etc.

- **Partnerships:** Al-Qaeda's talents for creating alliances have transcended into state-sponsorship with nations with similar enemies. There are several examples, such as the alleged relationship with Iran (fostered in Sudan in the early 1990s). This partnership bridged the Sunni-Shia divide, and some believe it resulted in Iran's Revolutionary Guard supplying operational and financial support to Al-Qaeda.

I would like to finish this chapter by covering a legacy business system that needs to be mentioned: the humble meeting. Meetings can often be used as mechanisms to ensure that deadlines have been met, which means the meeting is commonly used as a motivational tool. If you do use a regular meeting in this fashion, why not also offer transparency in terms of the metrics that need to be met and cancel the meeting?

Meetings can be littered with attendees who are driven by a fear of missing out. This means they are scared that they we will be judged or forgotten if they do not accept every invite. In cultures where presence equates to productivity (effective presenteeism), then meetings serve as success inhibitors. In these scenarios, we all have a role to play in effecting change.

Attendance can also be perpetuated by the practice of blanket invites. These can be driven by an organiser when they feel they risk offending through omission, or even purposefully invite someone for the duration, when they know they will only contribute for a fraction. In these instances, time spent in preparation (two-way dialogue) is a very worthy investment.

I have been in many mandatory meetings where I have found myself convinced that I am the only one frustrated by its pointless nature. However, research suggests this is a common illusion and, when others share common feelings that are not collectively acknowledged, then it is termed pluralistic ignorance. This should be raised within any other business (AOB).

When we are consumed by one task (and under pressure to complete it), then the introduction of another task, no matter how counterproductive, can make us feel more productive and provide us with an 'excuse'. This is known as the Mere Urgency Effect and can result in our attendance at routine meetings with low yield. Take a breath and re-evaluate your day.

Finally, we can suffer meeting amnesia where the same topics are consistently revisited, but without any additional information or progress updates. This can be due to lack of structure (no previous synopsis/no forward-looking agenda), and invariably leads to disengagement. One of the first points of any meeting should be to recap the main points from the last.

The solution lies within a collaborative culture that encourages challenge. This is where the organiser considers the true 'cost' of the meeting, whilst the attendee questions the value of their attendance. Time and resources have never been so precious as they will be in the year ahead, and it would be a shame to sacrifice them in rooms where they do not belong.

In the meetings we do have, care must be taken to frame them correctly. Two pieces of valuable context: 1) An average workforce group will contain about 40% visual learners, another 40% of auditory learners, with the remaining 20% learning best by kinesthetics; 2) The 'forgetting curve' is a hypothesis that states, on average, 42% of information is lost after 20 minutes, 56% after an hour, 64% after nine hours and so on. One way to do this is to reformat them 'off the curve'.

The phrase 'zoom fatigue' is used to describe the tiredness that accompanies the overuse of virtual platforms, especially due to meetings. Unsurprisingly, the expression has recently grown in prominence. As much as the factors that shape the condition are cognitively sophisticated, the solutions do not need to be.

This story begins during a chat with my partner's brother. I enjoy talking to this exceptionally enigmatic and likeable guy, and it always spikes my interest when he mentions his work in the field of advertising. It was during this part of the conversation that I first heard mention of 'walking meetings'.

After a little research, and an encouraging conversation with my partner, I identified a suitable meeting in my own diary. The weekly meeting in question was used to discuss thc progress of departmental projects. I floated the idea with the management team, and we agreed to give it a shot.

Due to their willingness to try something new, that weekly meeting is now a walking experience. During last week's meeting, I walked 4,500 steps in the fresh air whilst enjoying the views of my favourite weekend walk. Not only did this elevate my mood, but it did so without inbox 'pings' or screen distractions.

We have a duty to create a healthy working environment, as well as one that fulfils business objectives. This example achieved both. The department in question now looks forward to a meeting that is interesting, breaks up their working day and alleviates 'zoom fatigue'. Walking meetings are just one thing that we can do to redefine a legacy practice that 83% of managers rate as 'unproductive'.

In conclusion to this chapter, don't underestimate the favourable impact of ESG on the workings of a business risk profile, or the importance of identifying and committing to your organisation's core businesses. However, be careful not to let your concentration on those areas of the business blinker you from innovation and relevance within your market. Lastly, if change is required, which is generally the case, then choose to proactively manage it to your advantage, rather than hoping it will positively resolve itself (it won't), and try not to hold too many meetings along the way!

Chapter Four

Decision-Making (& Error), Delegation & Risk

'We all make choices, but in the end, our choices make us.'

—Ken Levine

Since the beginning of my career, I have been fortunate enough to travel extensively. It even got to the stage where I would apply for new passports, not because their validity had elapsed, but due to there either being no pages left for new stamps or I had 'unfriendly' stamps that raised red flags with various border controls that either wasted operational time or caused me to miss connections.

I do not travel so much anymore (and I miss that sometimes), but I certainly use my current job to 'stay in touch' with the world scene. I do this in several ways, one of which is monitoring a range of data points from sources I have judged to be relevant and reliable. Specifically, this is done in relation to places and/or sectors where my company or clients have a vested interest.

I really enjoy this aspect of threat identification, and the subsequent risk forecasting allows me to recall my own boots-on-ground experience to provide priceless context, as well as jogging various memories that range from the mind-numbingly mundane to the downright outrageous.

In today's world, what I am now seeing are elements (more than I have ever seen before) that we should all be collectively concerned about. This is no secret and has caused many businesses in all sectors to actively monitor their threat horizon. What they are seeing is an increasing variety of known and emerging risks, all of which are growing in both severity and frequency.

This has led to reinvestment in resilience processes, which has resulted in a plethora of entities who are (on paper, but rarely functionally tested) agile, and possess the capability and capacity to change operating models in line with hostile market conditions.

However, as much as it would appear that risk appetites and tolerances are changing, I am also seeing evidence that many firms are dangerously fixated on short-term macro-economic issues. This is especially the case with those organisations that have also deemed their business managers to be risk managers, without any meaningful training.

This has resulted in many medium- to long-term risks, ranging from supply chain vulnerability to geopolitical crisis, to continue approaching like a freight train (but under the radar of most). This is because they cannot be recognised by someone with a limited amount of textbook and training time. The risk constantly changes and evolves by being pushed and pulled by countless interlinked and autonomous, internal, and external influences within a massive ecosystem of consideration.

In terms of this topic, and in respect to the rise of activism, let's talk about the security of personnel and the role of threat intelligence. I wanted to do this due to a small number of fatal attacks that have been made on British politicians in recent years, and the prospect of that risk in relation to commercial figures.

Threat intelligence is knowledge that allows you to prevent or mitigate attacks by making informed and pragmatic risk-based decisions. To be effective, that decision must be actionable, timely, include relevant context, and be understood by key enablers and decision-makers.

Therefore, when threat intelligence is not fully integrated within a wider personnel security decision envelope, it can result in dangerous vulnerabilities. This is because effective protection can only be as good as the risk modelling that anticipates threat actors, their tactics, enemy techniques, etc.

Risk modelling is based upon the premise that we accept that there is always going to be a threat landscape, and so we identify and prioritise what is in it. This kind of transparency in the threat environment adds layers of resilience and recovery, should the proactive measures fail. We can divide this transparency into three sub-categories:

- **Strategic:** Provides a broad overview of a threat landscape for a specific organisation. It informs high-level decisions and is not technical. This provides insight into certain lines of action, broad patterns in threat actor tactics and targets, geopolitical events, trends, etc.

- **Tactical:** Outlines the tactics, techniques, and procedures (TTPs) and is used to understand the attack vectors that a threat actor may use. It includes technical context and is unique to an organisation, and therefore is only used by those directly responsible for the defence of the business.
- **Operational:** Knowledge about attacks, events, campaigns, etc. It aids response teams to understand the nature, intent, and timing of specific attacks, and how to defend against them.

Reliable threat intelligence helps identify and manage the vulnerabilities which pose a real risk. It enables you to base your decisions on real-time credible threats so that you can navigate your risk environment. The simple truth is, if you are prominent and not working with a protection specialist, then make no mistake about it: you present as an underprepared, vulnerable, and attractive target.

If we stick with decision-making, I do not think it would be a huge surprise to anyone to learn that our brains have evolved cognitive shortcuts (heuristics). What may be a surprise to some is that these neural pathways between our neocortex ('thinking brain') and amygdala ('survival brain') detract from our rational thought.

The most likely reason the brain does this is to nudge uncertainty (unknown unknowns) into risks (known unknowns). This means that when we are presented with an 'unknown', our brain accesses a library of existing patterns within our memories and overlays the closest match as a best guess (the brain loves patterns).

This recollective process eases the cognitive load (an advantage in an increasingly complex world), but also means the trade-off between an optimum result and a satisfactory outcome is often made in our unconscious minds. Have you ever thought, 'Why didn't I see that? It was so obvious in retrospect'?

If you have had those thoughts, then you are most likely the subject of hindsight bias; but, there will be a chance you did not 'see' the right choice because your striatum (another brilliant part of your brain) had 'sold' another, more familiar, reality (that you had seen before) to your consciousness.

Repeating these heuristics causes them to become engrained, and we create meaningful filters in our perspective that are commonly referred to as bias. For example:

- **Confirmation bias** is a tendency to favour that which conforms to an existing belief.
- **Attentional bias** is a tendency to solely focus on certain information.
- **Anchoring bias** is a tendency to rely on the first piece of information that was offered.

One solution for a company would be to initiate training that goes beyond process and teaches decision-making. This would have to be an immersive experience that left no doubt when ethical priorities take precedence over prescriptive direction, because not everything fits neatly in a procedure.

There is a story about Leonardo Da Vinci that focuses on ethical actions and distils down into the fable that he used to buy all the caged birds that he walked past, because he felt compelled to set them free as he could not stand seeing such beauty confined.

Beyond his endearingly unique personal traits, when he was not busy inventing flying machines or developing solar power, Da Vinci was gifting the world with works of art like the Mona Lisa and delivering timeless quotes such as, 'Simplicity is the ultimate sophistication'. Quite the character!

In terms of decision-making, the benefit of a simplistic approach is rarely realised within an alarmingly sophisticated world. This is not helped by human emotional complexities in a progressively information-rich and connected working landscape. One tactic is to encompass the process in a game.

Game Theory gives a simplified format where the strategic interactions among rational decision-makers can be analysed. If this analysis is done logically and accurately, then the outcomes can be calculated upon a probabilistic basis to the benefit (and inevitable loss) of the player sets.

This strategy is primarily used by economists, which is no doubt why eleven game theorists have won the Nobel Memorial Prize in Economic Sciences. The study begins with zero-sum gains (the winner wins what the loser loses) within two types: those which are cooperative and those which are non-cooperative (or competitive).

Both cooperative and competitive games are played with symmetric (similar strategies by both players) and/or asymmetric (players employ differing strategies) aspects, with either perfect or imperfect information sets (relating to the level of knowledge of previous moves).

Cooperative games centre around the formation (and behaviour) of alliances and is where we meet the **Shapley Value**. The Shapley Value is a mathematical mechanism which attempts to quantify the importance of a player by calculating their marginal contribution to define what is fair remuneration.

It was almost certainly a derivative of the Shapley Value that was used to calculate your wages (with varying degrees of success within most organisations), and it is the mechanism that good leaders use to decide upon resource allocation (particularly in the case of investment in the development of key personnel).

The other side of the coin contains 'competitive' games, and these are incredibly interesting. These games possess **the famous prisoner dilemma**, which is an exceptional quandary in which the potential custodial sentences of two alleged criminals are considered.

For me, the prisoner dilemma is not about binary risk/reward calculations, but an insight into behavioural economics regarding trust and contention. These are dependent upon gaining the fabled **Nash Equilibrium**, a set of 'no lose' circumstances (like a 'checkmate' scenario).

So, to capitalise upon the simplicity of a game to steer us towards our own Shapley Value, whilst positioning the Nash Equilibrium within easy reach, it is easier to 'play' the decisions rather than 'live' them. This was one of the reasons why I enjoyed studying economics, because it provided me with a rational way to explain the world and, as someone who makes a living dealing in uncertainty, that is golden.

During the pandemic, it was interesting, certainly not surprising, to watch the macro and micro models expand and contract under the direct and indirect influence of the virus. Regardless of what the political rhetoric claimed at the time, it was not 'unprecedented', but was a series of very predictable economic cycles that were travelling well-worn paths. It would be fascinating to have questioned the pandemic decision-makers about their game strategy.

For example, perhaps it could have been gamed that the rapid switch from pre-pandemic austerity to the release of a post-COVID global stimulus package totalling $10.4trn resulted in demand outstripping supply and headlines about empty shelves and dry fuel pumps. Similar trends have permeated to most industries. This provides proof that our own supply chains are subject to an expansion coefficient that can only be stretched so far before it snaps and becomes our equivalent of the 'empty shelves' (certainly not a Nash Equilibrium).

However, gamification is not always as easy as it sounds, and this lesson highlights the importance of assurance activities to validate that all parties within a project, especially those outsourced, can still deliver their scope of work should a reasonably foreseeable event occur. Another interesting example of a more dynamic type of assessment was completed during WWII when the US Navy was losing an unsustainable number of aircraft.

At that time, it was thought that extra armour was the answer. However, more armour meant more fuel and it also adversely affected manoeuvrability, which meant the aircraft would be more susceptible to enemy fighters. Therefore, it was imperative for the US Navy to find the optimum placement of armour that offered the highest survivability whilst adding the least weight.

To solve this conundrum, the US military turned to an Austro-Hungarian mathematician called Abraham Wald, who had moved to America before WWII and subsequently joined the Statistical Research Group (SRG). The SRG was a research group at Columbia University that solved military problems using mathematics.

Wald soon concluded, from the data he was given, that the distribution of bullet holes revealed that the fuselage and wings of a plane were hit most often. When Wald made this finding public, it was naturally expected that he would advise the military to reinforce these areas with armour. However, Wald advised the opposite, to put the armour where the bullet holes were absent.

His rationale was that the data had come from aircraft that had been able to return to base, and so did little more than to prove where the planes had increased resilience. He argued that bullet holes were not seen in the engines because those aircraft had been destroyed by enemy fire.

Wald's advantage was pattern recognition and a tendency towards the abstract. Wald took the time to diligently visit each variable in turn and, when he reduced the probability of engine damage affecting airworthiness to zero, he was left with two outcomes. The first was that bullets never hit the engines (unlikely, considering the integrity of the air frame), with the second being that the engine was the essential point of vulnerability that led to catastrophic failure.

Whilst both scenarios were undeniably possible and explained the data, there was only one that was realistic. Wald had recognised what the military had not, that the answer lay in the shadows of **survivorship bias**. Therefore, contrary to the immediate conclusions, the enemy fire was tolerated in the fuselage and wings, and the engines therefore received more armoured.

These methodologies and philosophies are still in use today, with the American A-10 'Warthog' close air support (CAS) airframe being a famous example:

Where Wald did not see bullet holes (the engines): Two armoured TF34-GE-100 turbofan engines compartmentalised by firewalls and fire extinguishers. All four fuel tanks are separate to the fuselage with self-sealing lines (and check valves) and, if all four tanks are lost, two self-sealing sumps containing enough fuel for another 230 miles of flight.

Where Wald saw bullet holes (fuselage and wings): Double-redundant hydraulics, with mechanical backups, and can fly with one engine, half a tail, and half a wing.

These examples work as a reminder that, in the analysis of risk, it is vital that we challenge assumptions and look beyond the obvious 'bullet holes'. So, whilst the world continues to accelerate away from any previous 'norm', how do we manage the increase of known unknowns and unknown unknowns within our existing risk frameworks?

A risk register underpins an organisation with risk descriptions, owners, types (business, operational, etc.), likelihoods, severity, status, and measures to either prevent, mitigate and/or transfer risk. The document is derived using generic hazard identification methodologies which measure positive and negative risk against its potential interface with interested parties. ISO defines an 'interested party' as 'those who affect or can be affected'. For example: employees, clients, suppliers, regulators, pressure groups, etc.

To do this, I tend to begin with a PESTLE (political, economic, social, technological, environmental, and legal) which I combine with a SWOT (strength, weaknesses, opportunities, and threats). By using both methodologies in unison, an organisation can populate their risk register and create their own unique risk profile (appetite versus capacity versus requirement).

By doing so, the company adds meaningful perspective to their strategy and objectives – which, in turn, informs vision and mission. In times of change, an organisation can live and die by a risk register. The secret to having an accurate risk register is matching the management of the document (frequency and competency of review) with the threat landscape and hazard burden.

This is where a risk management professional pays for themselves many times over, by ensuring that the register is current and matching the contents with usable quantitative risk probability. There are several proven methods that can help you to accurately quantify risk; these range from sensitivity examinations (often seen as a tornado diagram) to expected monetary value (EMV) analyses (commonly used in decision trees). However, what all quantitative methods deliver are verifiable data sets that leaders can employ to make objective decisions.

It is by following this journey map (or something relatively close) that resilience can be built through solid business continuity management (BCM) practices. This is because, without the hazards from a PESTLE being fed into a SWOT and captured in a register with assigned probabilities, your business impact assessments (BIA) can only be subjective guesswork that is hugely subject to error.

In terms of error, there is a growing body of research that suggests it is not actually a human problem, but is far more closely related to symptoms of wider organisational weakness. If we re-examine human performance through this refreshing lens, then the uncomfortable truth is that we are responsible for building error traps into work processes that we then hold others accountable for falling into.

This thinking is based on research that has logically concluded that unplanned events rely on such a vast number of precursors that causation could not lie at the door of a sole human. Pragmatism would, therefore, dictate that, to reduce the likelihood of human error, we would be best to spend our resources on error-proofing our organisational systems, of which our people are only a part.

In terms of errors, there are skill-based errors that involve memory tasks and account for 25% of the total, rule-based errors that account for 60% and involve technical know-how (deviating from a procedure), and knowledge-based (a reliance on perception) errors, which are thought responsible for the remaining 15%. What is interesting is that causation commonalities exist in them all: high stress; pushing beyond human capability; sophisticated systems, etc.

When we accept that those reoccurring aspects play a key role in facilitating unplanned events, then we can move to design organisation systems that prevent them, or at least mitigate the occurrence of dangerous assumptions, bias, etc. What this would potentially look like would be integrated work planning, where the likes of condition-based equipment maintenance would be given the same spotlight as performance-based human ability and competence (but today's world is far more in favour of the equipment).

Ultimately, this approach involves accepting that 'to err is human', and then addressing the preconditions of the 'err'. This requires building a just culture where blame is replaced by learning within a growth philosophy. So, prior to prescriptive augmentative technology showing the way, simply building healthy and educated attitudes based on professional integrity is key to reducing human error frequency.

We can say that the reduction of human error frequency is an instinctive Darwinian must; and, as such, we have become very adept at dynamically assessing the world around us so that we can pair risk with rational action (your existence proves that). When we get it right, our subjective risk levels match an objective risk requirement, and we are safe and enjoy predictability, with the opposite being likely true if we make a mistake.

Unfortunately, this relatively straightforward equation is anything but simple, because our propensity for risk is a moving target that is dependent on everything from genetic disposition to sleep cycle. We also tend to normalise danger, which is especially true when we do not witness a negative outcome within a specified period involving a scenario we had previously labelled as 'risky'.

This trait means we continually adjust (our previously rational) actions to incrementally increase our risk exposure towards an impending failure. This is commonly known as the **Peltsman Effect**, which can be seen in action when drivers compensate for safety mechanisms (such as seat belts, anti-lock braking, etc.) with riskier behaviour.

The converse of the Peltsman Effect is also true and could be seen when the traffic incident rates fell dramatically in both Sweden and Iceland immediately after they switched from driving on the left of the road to the right. However, within 18 months the complacency grew, and maladjusted driver behaviour caused the incident rates to return to pre-change levels.

Peltsman subsequently concluded that regulation and the comfort of safety were both catalysts for 'risk compensation'. This was also the basis of Hyman Minsky's work, which stated that market 'stability begets instability' as, the longer a market is stable, the more comfortable investors will be with taking risk (one of the principles behind a boom-and-bust cycle).

So, if we know that humans miscalibrate probabilities, then the question must be how do we align confidence with judgement? The evidence would point us towards cultivating a chronic sense of unease. I am by no means saying that we should live in fear, but the odd reality check can be a healthy thing (and more productive than creating yet another barrier on one of Reason's diagrams).

Many of the points covered in this chapter have led safety and risk thought leaders to move on from the traditional thinking, that loss events are prevented by ensuring as few things as possible go wrong, and towards a performance focus (almost an All Black philosophy) that involves accounting for how (imperfect) people adjust for workplace changes (complexity, uncertainty, ambiguity, conflicts, etc.).

It is undeniable that there is a compelling case for the application of 'people science' principles, especially in a form that best accounts for the operational, industrial, commercial, and cultural landscape. Perhaps this is the right time to introduce an unfortunately tragic real-world example, as follows.

On 19 June 2013, at the 'Piper 25' Oil & Gas UK Conference in Aberdeen, the Hon. Sir Charles Haddon-Cave delivered a speech entitled 'Leadership & Culture, Principles & Professionalism, Simplicity & Safety – Lessons from the Nimrod Review'. The Nimrod Review was a result of the loss of RAF Nimrod XV230 over Afghanistan on 2 September 2006. This event resulted in the death of all 14 service personnel onboard the aircraft.

The investigation found that, within 90 seconds of the Nimrod completing air-to-air refuelling with a Tristar, fire warnings in the bomb bay and elevator bay sounded. The aircraft quickly depressurised, and flames were seen on the starboard engines. A Mayday was issued and the flight diverted to Kandahar. At 3,000 feet, six minutes after the first warning, the aircraft exploded. The cause was not enemy fire, but leaking fuel ignited by a hot cross-feed pipe.

During the speech, Sir Charles recounted his investigation with the humble professionalism that you would expect. He gave expert insight into several critical areas, but the part of his speech that stuck with me throughout the years was his 'Seven Lessons from Nimrod', which can be used in a proactive or reactive fashion:

- **Look at the underlying organisational causes:** It is easy to blame the person holding the hammer, but it is vital to examine the 'organisational causes' that allowed the failure.
- **Beware assumptions:** It was assumed the plane was safe because it had a complex system, a Safety Case outsourced to the original manufacturer, and 30 years of flight.
- **Avoid change for change's sake:** Change can become addictive and will distract and disrupt people from doing their day job, and can be as dangerous as it is wasteful.
- **Avoid the comfort of complexity, compliance & consensus:** Complexity is an enemy of safety, compliance involves process (not problem), and consensus leads to obedience.

- **If you must outsource, do not to outsource your thinking:** The quick fix to remove head count from the balance sheet can be corrosive to competence, culture, and memory.
- **A Safety Case should be an aid to thinking, not an end to it:** Generally, 'paper safety' that is unusably big and lacks operator input, but provides some excellent 'shelf-ware'.
- **Age matters:** Older equipment needs greater rigor, resources, and vigilance with the right resources, priorities, and attention to detail to collect data, trends, and patterns.

The lesson is that we do not seem to find new ways to create loss; we seem intent on repeating mistakes and suffering the same tragic outcomes. Sir Charles' speech went on to cover several other areas of interest, one of which provides a poignant way to finish this chapter. He linked each of the seven Nimrod themes (above) to past incidents, such as the Space Shuttle Challenger (1986) and Columbia (2003), Zeebrugge (1987), King's Cross Fire (1987), the Marchioness (1989) and the BP Texas City (2005).

In conclusion to this chapter, do not underestimate your vulnerability to errors and the value in threat intelligence (far beyond personal security) and risk modelling. Be self-aware enough to actively mitigate heuristics in yourself and your team, so that you can effectively delegate, recognise the Shapley Value and position yourself in a 'no lose' Nash Equilibrium, whilst also building layers of resilience (just in case).

Chapter Five

Resilience, Response & Continuity

'She stood in the storm and when the wind did not blow her way, she adjusted her sails.'

–Elisabeth Edwards

On a cold and clear day on 15 January 2009, Captain Chelsey 'Sully' Sullenberger was onboard US Airways Flight 1549, approximately 3000ft above New York facing an unprecedented crisis, having lost engine power due to a bird strike. The decisions he took in the ensuing 208 seconds decided the fate of all 155 souls onboard. Sully took control from his co-pilot, broadcast a Mayday, told his co-pilot to initiate the engine restart procedure, and began to dynamically assess emergency landing options.

In short order, he took the decision to land on the nearby Hudson river. Those actions and that decision proved instrumental in an outcome with no loss of human life. It was later proven by the investigators that any other course of action would have ended in disaster. All aspects were examined, and it was found that Sully never raised his voice or hesitated with his actions. He was a perfect exemplar of calm, decisive leadership that, I am glad to say, is rarely tested beyond the simulator.

Almost 30 years before (December 1978), United Airlines Flight 173 was seconds away from landing at Portland International Airport when Captain Malburn McBroom's warning lights indicted a catastrophic landing gear failure. Captain McBroom acted decisively by taking control of the aircraft, alerting air traffic control and aborting. McBroom then calmly put the aircraft into a holding pattern and prepared the passengers and emergency services for a potential crash landing.

Flight 173 destroyed two houses and several acres of woodland when it ran out of fuel and crashed. Due to some exceptional flying by McBroom, only 10 out of the 189 lives onboard were lost; he was later stripped of his pilot's licence and quietly retired. McBroom spent too long deliberating and his distraction resulted in the aircraft running out of fuel. It was agreed by many that both pilots were competent, decisive, and good under pressure, but McBroom simply didn't have the time to delegate.

Even though McBroom had engineers, stewards, and a co-pilot, he attempted to fix the landing gear, brief passengers, and fly the plane. His micromanagement was instrumental in losing track of time and fuel. When we look at Sully's situation, we see a different picture. He had his co-pilot work on the engines whilst his cabin crew dealt with the passengers, which left him free to concentrate on the only thing that mattered – how to land the plane without loss of life.

These stark examples caused a fundamental change in pilot training. Whereas McBroom's highly directive approach had been encouraged prior to his crash, the change was to encourage controlled autonomy, as per Crew Resource Management (CRM) principles. In essence, CRM is concerned with the interpersonal skills and leadership that focus on actions during routine flying, in the belief that crisis performance hinges upon the culture created by that leader before the crisis was apparent.

This lesson can also be transferred to our management systems, which are based on a flawed assumption of organisational theory in that there is a certain level of predictability in our world. This Newtonianesque train of thought encourages simplification to bring order and is why management systems are considered as the be all and end all, because they make sense and fit in a 'box'.

Problems begin when circumstances become complex and outpace such a one-dimensional framework. This was ably demonstrated by the COVID-19 pandemic. In these instances, the framework requires a system that can stretch beyond the obvious, to assimilate context. This means re-examining the complexity science that underpins the current way CMS are built, to reveal a next generation approach. In practice, this multi-dimensional perspective would involve the creation of 'streams' that would exist on a sliding scale from simple to sophisticated:

- **Simple** would heavily encapsulate process-oriented situations with clear cause-and-effect relationships that primarily use 'known knowns'. This would involve straightforward directives giving proven outcomes by means of easily delegated functions. This vanilla thinking has produced the vast majority of today's CMS, all constructed to similar standards regardless of the complexity of the operations/organisation/interfaces/industries they face.

- **Sophisticated** would be characterised by less-mapped and more ambiguous scenarios where the investigation of 'known unknowns' is done, whilst simultaneously formulating multiple solutions based on changing priorities and constantly evolving consequences. This type of framework would ensure that nothing was missed and would suit business continuity models.

By benchmarking the construct of a CMS on such a scale, it would increase resilience and reduce risk profile by facilitating an ability to immediately self-assess a conundrum into the appropriate stream. This would mean the time taken to begin meaningful action to address an issue (often called 'analysis paralysis') does not have to endure someone being forced to decide the right course, especially when influenced by unpredictability.

For example, in terms of emergency response analysis paralysis, the loss of the Alexander L. Kielland mobile offshore drilling unit (MODU) on 27 March 1980 will be remembered as one of the darkest days in offshore history. Only 89 of the 212 personnel onboard survived that day, with 123 souls perishing in cold waters.

At the time of the disaster, the MODU was being used as an accommodation 'flotel' for the production platform Edda 2/7C. The 14 minutes between initial failure and eventual capsize left a window of time within which personnel could have escaped, had an effective command structure been in place.

Temperatures of 7°C in the air and 4°C in the sea meant the water was not a place to be. Four of the seven lifeboats were launched, and only two of the MODU's 20 rafts were launched and no one was rescued by the standby vessel *Silver Pit*, which took an hour to reach the scene.

The uncomfortable truth is that established CMS frameworks have done little to help us evolve in terms of emergency response or resilience. These tick-box clipboard exercises encourage ordered domains, asking little more than if a procedure exists (one dimensional), but doing very little in terms of giving any meaningful attention to construct (the next dimension).

Organisations should consider taking the time to reassess their CMS to ensure it has the capacity and capability to appropriately reflect their operational envelope in the modern world. The threat landscape has changed, and it has devalued much of the international certification we have previously coveted, meaning we can no longer rely on natural talent in unordered contexts.

Similar issues can be seen within the corporate structure, with the business case for a full-time crisis manager rarely being approved. What tends to happen is that an existing manager has crisis-related roles and responsibilities written into their 'normal' function.

This decision makes sense at the outset because, even in the absence of any notable crisis pedigree, the person's current role would logically mean that they are regarded as one of the company's most dependable assets. This invariably results in a crisis command structure that dangerously mirrors the everyday operational hierarchy.

This corporate trend has resulted in a contingent of part-time, well-meaning, well-trained, and well-respected crisis managers. However, they could not be termed 'competent'. The crux of the matter being that the developmental journey that was taken to earn their 'stripes' in their chosen discipline, has not then been followed with a commensurate journey within crisis management.

This presents several issues, not least because the skills of a business manager are a far reach from those of a crisis manager. This dichotomy amplifies when the cognitive loading and pressures of a crisis are applied in real time. In that instance, an individual will commonly revert to 'type', as they are most comfortable displaying the actions and behaviours that they have known to bring them previous (business) success.

This is usually manifested in things like decision-by-committee and departmental (wide) thinking. This contrasts with a crisis manager who will reduce spheres of influence and shorten decision lines by purposely directing one down, whilst simultaneously considering two down. This type of strategic and tactical thinking (running in parallel) is critical to foster the agility needed to keep 'the initiative' and bring solutions.

It is also inherently difficult for a business manager to come to terms with the unpredictable nature of a crisis. The sheer pace, combined with the sometimes unstoppable momentum, and the absence of any kind of linear predictability, takes many by surprise.

Those of us who are more experienced will remember our own 'rabbit in the headlights' moment(s) when we landed with a 'bang' to realise that the crisis was the one in control. To prevent this, what is required is the ability to combine unwavering focus with the innovative entrepreneurial skills required to engineer effective solutions. This is referred to as 'disciplined initiative' within military circles and takes extensive practice to become proficient, and complete dedication to be termed a 'professional'.

Managers also have a habit of over-complicating the planning aspect, due to the belief that it is comparable to generic strategy plans. Within a crisis, simplicity is king, and the call of the day is simple, clear, and timely instruction on four aspects: 1) the problem, 2) the information, 3) the options and 4) the solution(s).

During a crisis, it is commonly said that 80% of a plan delivered on time is preferable to a completed plan that is late. This is because it is highly unlikely that any plan will survive first contact with the enemy and, as Mike Tyson said, 'Everyone has a plan until they get punched in the mouth.' The lesson here is that the quality rests in the people, not the process (which should always stay fluid).

The manager must not succumb to their instinct of getting 'caught up'. In a crisis, it is essential to be able to step back and overlay near-term objectives with long-term visions. This skill facilitates the capability to direct the immediate situation, whilst simultaneously de-risking the next steps.

This is also difficult for managers who, depending upon their leadership style, feel threatened or undermined by the performance of junior staff members. In a crisis, there is no room for this type of petty distraction; there must be an understanding that rank does not matter, that it is all about the mission.

Traditionally, there were only a small number of individuals that were taught to manage undesirable emotions, fear being one. This niche education had been associated with sports until the early 1990s, at which time the penny dropped within the military that there was little difference, on a physiological level, between preparing to kick down an insurgency-held door and preparing to take a penalty kick.

This led to 'stress inoculation' within military training, which translated into conditioning against fear by consistent exposure to extreme battlefield conditions. This allowed fear normalisation, within which personnel could acknowledge the emotion, and then either suppress it (by breathing, self-talking, compartmentalisation, etc.) or replace it with more useful responses that capitalise on things like excitement, loyalty, etc.

Within these situations, the body was found to initiate several involutory processes, including vasoconstriction, where blood is removed from the surface and stored in arteries and the core to ensure vital organ function and prevent bruising. This process also removes certain functionality from the brain and invariably results in a lack of rational thought.

It is in this space that someone can be successfully taught to perform under extreme pressure, and is why modern military training 'almost' guarantees that every soldier will return fire when engaged by an enemy. However, as time passes, there will be performance degradation unless the required act (be that firing a weapon, or directing an emergency response team) is practised to the point of automation.

Therefore, emergency response drills are critical to ensure that all personnel are as acclimatised as possible to the stresses of an actual event. With that in mind, and with the thought that paralyses and/or panic costs lives in an emergency, give your own emergency response drills the respect that they deserve. I understand that we are generally not door kickers nor goal kickers, but let's try harder and take the time and effort required to prepare our personnel for the reasonably foreseeable.

No doubt it is exciting to watch characters in tense Hollywood movies make life or death decisions based on 'gut' but, unsurprisingly, the reality of a crisis manager is a little more calculated. Crisis leadership boils down to the ability to dynamically assess a range of cause-and-effect probabilities which, in tandem with a consideration of likelihood and impact, fuel informed decisions to choose the best path to a desired outcome.

The mindset must remain constantly agile, as risk-based thinking is contextual and dependent upon simultaneously understanding, anticipating, and prioritising (relevant) current and potential macro and micro circumstances. The very nature of crisis leadership presents multiple options in a reduced timeframe, all of which have a unique risk and reward footprint.

High-performance teams often rely on empowering the judgement of a boots-on-ground leader to make the best call. Thankfully for those in command, this also involves the transfer of risk which alleviates the burden of command and is often talked of as the leader's 'absorb, delegate or elevate' decision process.

It is also important to appreciate that judgement is influenced by an instinct to adopt a defensive approach. However, the role of a crisis leader is to take calculated risks to exploit opportunities, and risk aversion has been proven time and again to often be the most dangerous default. This means the leader must be aware of risk tolerance to ensure that rational analysis is not replaced by reckless gambling.

It is a mistake to think that emergency response arrangements are fit for purpose because your hardware reaches a performance standard; the people matter, too. It is also a mistake to think that someone who is a good 'peacetime' leader is a competent crisis leader (think Churchill in reverse).

I accepted an invitation to present at an energy industry health & safety forum to talk about many of these aspects. I chose to go there with my 'crisis manager' hat on (it fits best) and talk about the role that predictive analysis plays in resilience planning.

I took the opportunity to talk the attendees through the application of business continuity techniques that have proven to minimise the organisational impact of disruptive events. I chose this subject because I believe contemporary 'safety' can often be little more than the reactive commercialisation of failures and incidents, leaving the moral imperative involved in prevention unintentionally missed. Please do not misunderstand me; of course I see the value in retrospective learning, but we must also look forward to preparing for what is coming.

With that in mind, I highlighted to the group what I believe to be the top five global threats in terms of likelihood and severity. Within that ranking, I put geoeconomic confrontations at the top, and justified this by outlining the indictors and sources that informed my rationale. My conclusion was that this type of conflict presents the largest medium- to long-term threat that we collectively face as a global community, certainly in the coming decade. Beyond that, it looks likely that climate science may result in me putting a different global threat at number one.

If I am right concerning conflict, and I hope I am not, then we must prepare for a landscape that has not been seen since the last Cold War. We know that burying our heads in the sand is no longer an option; Russia has shown us just how closely we are all anchored to conflict. So, with that in mind, here are five topics you may want to consider within your own resilience plans:

1. **Business:** Decision-makers must have a functional understanding of geopolitical issues, and access to a process that yields an aggregate company view/stance. There are several off-the-shelf products that can do this, or you could

develop an organisation-specific scorecard that includes all the essentials relevant to your business (legal, security, finance, logistics, etc.).

2. **Reputation:** There must be strong internal alignment on activities connected to, or potentially impacted by, geopolitical challenges. This could involve market-specific assessments which merge strategy with risk, or even the communication of an outright stance. This narrative can then be communicated to interested parties so the market can truly understand the brand.
3. **Operational:** The vulnerability of a range of topics from supply chain pinch points to trade protectionism should nudge the organisation to take a two-pronged approach: developing the strength to protect processes, whilst retaining the agility to pivot to alternate arrangements. This means re-evaluating just-in-time by investing in potentially expensive redundancy.
4. **Technology:** Organisations must face up to the challenge of maintaining global networks, particularly in countering the 'splinternet'. Companies must ensure they comply with local data management requirements (such as GDPR) and learn how to safely compartmentalise data (for security purposes) whilst also preserving performance and user experience.
5. **Financial:** Many have lost out due to the link of conflict with currency fluctuations, market activity and sanctions which, on occasion, lead to expropriation. These are now navigated in a global economy with other macro challenges such as cross-continent inflation and the intent of some to weaponise certain industries (with energy being the prime example).

The above exercise only relates to geoeconomic confrontations (conflict), but many of the fundamentals are relevant across the risk spectrum. This means it would be prudent to also consider digital inequality/vulnerability, climate failure and biodiversity loss, debt crises and ongoing pandemic impacts (social erosion, mental health deterioration, etc.).

When doing this analysis, the principles of business continuity management (BCM) give special focus to the link between a business impact assessment (BIA) and risk assessment (RA). I firmly believe that the interdependence of these two aspects creates the backbone of organisational resilience, and the following mechanism can be as fun as it is fascinating.

A BIA is a simple five-step process that is used to identify your key products and services and define the critical activities that you use to deliver them. It analyses the impact of disruption to these activities, and balances that against the resources that would be needed to resume activities:

1. A **competent quorum** lists the key products and services and notes the related potential impact from disruption.
2. This is **laid against a timeline** which then shows an evolving profile of the disruption against time-based benchmarks: immediate, up to 24 hours, 24–48 hours, one week, etc.
3. Plot the time that you are comfortable in **managing a disruption** to each product and service which identifies when each key product and service needs to resume.

4. Then reverse engineer the critical activities required to deliver the key products and services and **quantify the resources you need** for those critical activities.

You then need to conduct an RA that looks at the likelihood and impact from a variety of risks that have a realistic potential to cause the BIA disruptions. This means you will then be able to appropriately prioritise risk reduction activities. This involves seven, very simple steps.

1. **Compartmentalise** the critical parts of your business (staff, systems, premises, etc.).
2. Each of those factors then needs to be **paired with a likelihood** from the event in question.
3. Then **note down the arrangements** that are in place to prevent and reduce that likelihood.
4. **List anything else** that could further prevent and/or reduce the likelihood.
5. These 'further' measures must also then be **assigned a likelihood score**.

Now the meaningful link...

6. Use a **risk matrix to plot the likelihood** that you have now identified (Step 5) **against the impact** identified within the initial stages of your BIA.
7. Then **use the matrix to rank the risk** and assist you to decide to either:
    I. **treat** the risk with a BCM process
    II. **tolerate** it and do nothing

III. **transfer** to another party (insurance)

IV. **terminate** because of an intolerable risk/reward calculation.

I have just described one piece of a mechanism that I prefer to use, which will not necessarily be right for you. Anyone can create a good BCM system that is commensurate with their needs and appetite. However, you must respect the fact that BCM stretches beyond normal business processes and settles within the potentially dark and desperate world of Darwin and simple survival. So, if you are not sure of what you are doing, then call a professional.

The world is full of examples of why you would need competent advice. This is often the case when organisational or system complexity outstrips competence and control. This is often the case in relation to technology, which is why it is not surprising that spending on global cybersecurity is predicted to surpass $133 billion in 2022, which represents a 30-fold increase in the last 13 years.

In terms of the vulnerability to an exponentially increasing threat landscape, in 2017 Equifax provided an example of a relatively simple hack via a consumer complaint web portal that had not been updated. Combined with poor data governance, it allowed the intruders over 76 days of undetected access. Impressively (in terms of resilience and recovery), Equifax regained full market cap resolution within two years.

We can certainly say that the startling rate of change within our world is unprecedented; never have global challenges arrived with such velocity and ferocity. The current recipe contains pandemics, a cost-of-living crisis, climate emergencies and escalating geopolitical tensions that have, certainly in one case, created a tragic humanitarian disaster that leaves many innocent people facing a long, dark, and cold winter.

These factors, individually and collectively, can unsettle and distress even the strongest character, especially when combined with a 'changing of the guard'. For example, in the UK in 2022, we suffered the loss of our Queen and said goodbye to a Prime Minister that, whether you liked him or not, provided consistent leadership throughout a pandemic that gave us all a stark reminder of our mortality (an aspect that was fuelled by a national media that revels in a 'click-bait' mentality).

If we then add into the mix the trials and tribulations of normal life (perhaps a child starting a new school term, or the loss of a loved one) combined with professional considerations (such as the implementation of a new IT system, or a valued colleague resigning), we can easily find ourselves caught in a whirlpool of circumstances that outpace our ability to 'cope'.

This comes in part from our innate inability to cope with the rate of change and unpredictability in today's world. This has translated into more risk, both perceived and real. It certainly feels like as soon as we breathe a sigh of relief on one event, another arrives to compound our anxiety. This cycle has the potential to breed frustration toward the present, and dread for the future. These feelings are natural and, to a degree, healthy. What follows are simple strategies that help us 'cope' during such times:

- **Catastrophising:** It is easy to fall into a cycle of catastrophic thinking, where the worst-case scenario is a 'go to'. It is important to interrupt these negative thought processes by staying cognisant of the fact that your negative thoughts are not necessarily representative of reality.
- **Activate your senses:** This distraction technique also works with physical pain and involves engaging in something that activates your senses. This type of stimulation centres a person within the moment (cooking, gardening, drawing, etc.) and lets us cathartically relax.
- **Talk and/or write:** Talking to a partner or a friend about our feelings can relieve stress and anxiety. We can get the same outcome by writing what we feel; this can also let us identify our thought patterns. Both methods are expressive and work against a 'bottled-up' stance.
- **Identify anxiety triggers:** We are creatures of habit, which allows us to identify the patterns that lead to our anxiety escalation. So, if we can derive the triggers, we can control exposure and mitigate their effect with sleep, a nutritious diet, exercise, connecting with nature, etc.
- **Doom-scrolling:** Social media amplifies anxiety and triggers existing underlying conditions such as feelings of isolation or insecurity. Limiting time on social media is a must in today's world to prevent being influenced by the mis- and disinformation on the various platforms.

- **Seek professional advice:** The way you are feeling could be justified and valid. We cannot be positive all the time. But, if feel your anxiety levels getting to an uncomfortable level, or they are causing unhealthy behaviours, then do not delay in reaching out to a professional.

It is important that we remember that we are all in this together, and we can reassure our personnel, and ourselves, that we are not alone. You are not the only one feeling the way you do, so do not be afraid to talk about it. Lastly, seeking professional help is like reaching for a glass of water – if you are thirsty, then you've waited too long, so take a drink before it's too late... And, if you need to talk, then do it. The alternative is unthinkable.

In turbulent times like these it is imperative that, as leaders, we can fall back on proven resilience techniques. An example of such is the Stockdale Paradox, something I first read about 20 years ago in Jim Collins' book *From Good to Great*. It is a concept born out of necessity almost 60 years ago by Admiral Jim Stockdale, the highest-ranking United States military officer to be detained in the 'Hanoi Hilton' Vietnamese prisoner-of-war camp. Stockdale believes that this technique was largely responsible for him emerging relatively unscathed from his eight-year imprisonment lasting from 1965 to 1973.

The methodology was first brought to the public's attention by Collins after reading *In Love and War*. In this book, written by Stockdale and his wife to document his captivity, Collins found himself reflecting and musing, 'I'm getting depressed reading this… if it feels depressing for me, how on earth did he deal with it when he was actually there and did not know the end of the story?'

When Collins was eventually able to ask Stockdale how he dealt with the horrors, brutality, and uncertainty of his captivity, the Admiral replied, 'I never lost faith in the end of the story. I never doubted not only that I would get out, but also that I would prevail in the end and turn the experience into the defining event of my life, which, in retrospect, I would not trade.'

Stockdale then highlighted it was the 'optimists' that were the most likely to succumb to the torturous conditions and not make it home. This is because they would become 'unglued when their predictions don't work out'. Stockdale qualified this by saying, 'You must never confuse faith that you will prevail in the end – which you can never afford to lose – with the discipline to confront the most brutal facts of your current reality, whatever they might be.' The Admiral went on to elaborate that he never planned for his release and lived 'day to day'.

If Admiral Stockdale were to talk to us today about the state of our world, he would no doubt tell us that change will come and go, and we should accept that there is very little we can do about that. However, what we can do is a) focus day by day and step by step (don't get ahead of ourselves), b) never shy away or run from the brutal facts, c) never lose faith that we will prevail in the end, and d) consistently provide an enduring, comforting, and realistic message to those that look up to us for guidance.

However, Admiral Stockdale also teaches us that not everyone can emerge unscathed from such a harrowing event. This can also be seen in other areas of crisis. For example, in 1998, approximately 10 years after the Piper Alpha disaster (1988), a group of academics tracked down 46 out of the 59 survivors. Their aim was to achieve a better understanding of what it means to survive a major disaster, and a total of 33 brave souls agreed to participate.

The majority were found to have been physically injured (83%), with 56% sustaining more than one injury, and 42% requiring hospital treatment. It came as no shock that psychological issues of some description were reported by 97% of the group, with 76% having had or were actively engaged in therapy; a further 55% were prescribed medication, 21% were involved in group psychotherapy, and 55% had a combination of some or all those treatments.

The study found that the most stringent diagnostic criteria for post-traumatic stress disorder (PTSD) was still met by 21% of the survivors over a decade later. That is not a surprise, when the majority (97%) stated that they had experienced the loss of a friend, 86% thought that they might die, and 56% witnessed someone being seriously injured or killed during the event.

Most survivors (61%) stated that the worst long-term effect was the impact on their emotional and psychological well-being, which then had a knock-on effect on their relationships. An incredible 61% showed staggering resilience by stating that some good had transpired from that fateful night, with 44% identifying a positive change in their emotional and personal life (e.g., felt closer to family, more emotionally expressive, and grateful for life).

These statistics are simply the tip of the iceberg and do nothing to examine the devastating impact that was, and will continue to be, felt within the families, communities, and groups of friends for generations to come. We all have a duty to remember what happened on 6 July 1988, and to ensure that those organisational and individual failings/errors are never repeated. What follows is a short reminder of what happened, and some of the lessons that should live with us every day of our careers:

6 July 1988 saw a series of explosions rip through the 34,000-ton Piper Alpha platform with the almost immediate loss of 167 lives. Amazingly, 61 souls survived, some of which did so by jumping as much as 175ft (53m) from the platform's helicopter deck into the burning sea.

The associated wells and lines ruptured and produced fires, with flames that reached 200 metres and had a peak consumption rate of ~100 gigawatts. That was three times the rate of the United Kingdom's total energy consumption. The platform was lost to sea within three hours, causing $3.4 billion of total insured damages and taking a further three weeks for the raging fire to be brought under control.

The uncomfortable truth is that several reports had predicted the event. One report (1986) concluded that a prolonged high-pressure gas fire would be impossible to fight, with another report (1987) highlighting the risks to personnel from platform abandonment, and yet another (1988) stating that the structural integrity of the entire platform could be lost by fire within 15 minutes. Unfortunately, the findings and recommendations of these reports were not acted on in time, and solutions such as the installation of sub-sea isolation valves and fireproofing were even labelled as impractical.

Disappointingly, there were also other warnings of institutional weaknesses within the safety management system on Piper Alpha. Less than a year earlier, on 7 September 1987, a rigger died in an incident on the platform, the investigation of which highlighted inadequacies in the permit to work system. Whether by direction or inaction, those vulnerabilities were not addressed. Failure within the permit to work system was later found to be a key contributing factor within the control of work system that made the initiation of the event possible.

One week after the disaster, Lord Cullen, a Senator of the College of Justice in Scotland, was appointed to hold a public inquiry. Piecing together what happened, why it happened and how to prevent a reoccurrence, took nearly two years and, due to most of the evidence resting at the bottom of the North Sea, the testimony of survivors and witnesses played a key role in creating a coherent timeline.

The comprehensive 400-page investigation report presented a detailed description of a catalogue of failures, early warnings and missed opportunities that were treated as either innocuous or did not give those in charge cause for concern. Lord Cullen's report set out a total of 106 recommendations, the responsibility for implementation of which was shared between the industry and the regulator. Even today, many of those recommendations are still relevant across all hazardous industries, from aviation to nuclear.

One of the most important lessons that Piper Alpha has taught us, is the importance of organisations associated with major accident hazards recognising that they have a greater potential for disastrous consequences that carry a higher potential cost in terms of lives and money. This means that those managing major hazards are duty-bound to aspire to a much higher standard of reliability than in normal commercial decision-making, and their arrangements must reflect that responsibility.

It is imperative that we collaborate within all industries to ensure that our work is built upon proven decision-making processes and solid engineering practices, that lower the risk of an unplanned event to as low as reasonably practicable (ALARP).

This is especially salient when we consider the paradigm shift within organisations that has been caused by COVID-19. The impact of the pandemic has commonly resulted in operating models that contain untested and unproven relationships, objectives, resource allocations, management systems, available expertise, engineering support, procurement, and so on.

In short, it has been proven beyond all reasonable doubt that it is very possible to recognise and prevent major accident causation anomalies before they escalate to a tragic chain reaction. That statement is not based upon the false economy of hindsight bias, but built on the foundations of too many instances of the worst type of loss.

Throughout my career, I have been involved in numerous investigations, ranging from criminal prosecutions to offshore oil rig fatalities (but nothing on the scale of Piper Alpha). I have also had the honour to lead several of those investigation teams, often during very trying times for all involved. The integrity of some of my team members over the years has been nothing short of humbling.

As a commercial investigation leader, you quickly get used to the fact you will not always be able to pick all the members of your team. This is because interested parties often (and understandably) insist that they have their own representatives within the group. Due to this, I always cover certain topics within my opening meeting with the investigation team, some of which I am meeting for the first time. This works very well on several levels, but ultimately it is so that we can all agree on the 'ground rules'.

There are quite a few topics on the menu of that conversation, such as the philosophies that we will use when investigating. This includes addressing the moral and ethical standards that we will (without question) uphold whilst conducting our business. This is essential for many reasons, not least due to the potential of a conflict of interest if we, for example, follow the evidence into areas that can expose those in positions of authority (such as our employers) to criticism. On the rare occasion that this happens, even the most robust moral compass is in danger of being knocked off course.

This conversation also gives me the chance to gauge competence, ensure the protection of critical processes (chain of evidence, etc.), and discover any predispositions (bias) a person may hold. It also enables me to agree the need for transparency in our confidence levels (rarely addressed in incident investigation courses) regarding our interpretation of a) the evidence, and b) what we believe it is telling us.

There are interesting legal nuances in this regard. For context, Scots Law requires the burden of proof in criminal cases to demonstrate guilt 'beyond reasonable doubt' (high confidence); whereas, civil cases only need a 'balance of probabilities' (51% decision). Now, imagine the different outcomes from an investigation process based only on absolutes (as is needed in criminal law), compared to that which also includes the 'most likely' (seen in civil cases).

Could we say that the two approaches would get the same root causes, or would the inclusion of the 'probable' dilute the process just too much? There is certainly no shortage of case history where this very thing has happened.

Therefore, when team members offer their conjecture into the process, it is important that they also feel comfortable enough to give the degree of confidence that they have in their offering. The group then uses that information within their decision criteria on the direction that they take the investigation (or launch sub-investigations that run in tandem to the main body of work). This is important, as an investigation may take a completely different turn when based on a definitive conclusion, compared to a working hypothesis.

An example of the enablers for indecision was given by the psychologist Elisabeth Loftus, who ably demonstrated the reliability of eyewitness testimony in 1974. She was testing if verbal cues could alter memory. She had 45 students watch a traffic accident film and then asked, ‘About how fast were the cars when they... into each other?’ The question was then completed with the words ‘smashed’, ‘collided’, ‘bumped’, ‘hit’ and ‘contacted’.

The results of the study showed that the use of action verbs altered the subject’s stated recollection of events. Those that heard ‘smashed’ estimated a speed of 40.8 mph, ‘collided’ 39.3 mph, ‘bumped’ 38.1 mph, ‘hit’ 34 mph, and ‘contacted’ 31.8 mph. This was deemed to be due to either 1) a response-bias influencing the answer, or 2) the memory footprint had been changed.

Loftus wanted to investigate this further, and so she gathered another 150 students and showed them another traffic accident film. The students were divided into three groups of 50. The first group was asked, ‘How fast were the cars going when they hit each other?’, those in the second group were asked, ‘How fast were the cars going when they smashed each other?’ and the third group was not questioned.

Loftus reinterviewed the students one week later and asked, ‘Did you see any broken glass in the film?’ Those who had been posed the question using the word ‘smashed’ were found more likely to report broken glass, despite no broken glass being in the original film. This is known as confabulation, when false memories are created with no recognition by the person.

This is just a small amount of research that casts doubt on eyewitness testimony. We could also talk about numerous other factors from environmental aspects to the forgetting curve (see Chapter Eight). However, the takeaway that I hope will resonate is that language really matters and, even if the interviewee is convinced they are correct, accuracy is never a guarantee.

This example highlights why the investigation leader must also give the reader of the investigation report an indication of the rationale behind the decisions that were made. This means we can only view an incident investigation report as one of many businesses improvement tools that a leadership team will use to base their strategic decisions.

For that reason, do not be discouraged if a report that contains no more than a fishbone and some recommendations is rejected and handed back to you with a request for more context. Just like your teacher said at school, it pays dividends to show your working (that is where you get the best marks).

I would like to visit a case study I did on the Battle of Mogadishu to finish this chapter on resilience, response, and continuity. This was a pivotal conflict that many are aware of via the lens of Ridley Scott in the film *Black Hawk Down*. As exceptional as that piece of cinema was, the following paragraphs may add a little context on the legacy that was left behind, and the role that leadership and resilience planning (or lack of) played in that.

Our focus begins in December 1992, which saw the US join the UN in Operation Restore Hope (Somali civil war). Then, in June 1993, 24 UN peacekeepers were killed, and a resolution was immediately passed to arrest those responsible. The prime suspect was a former general and the (then) current leader of the Somali National Alliance (SNA), Mohamed Farrah Aidid.

Aidid was a highly intelligent and strategic opponent. He had the benefit of formal law enforcement training at an infantry school in Rome, and was then selected to study advanced postgraduate military science at the Frunze Military Academy in the Soviet Union (an elite institution reserved for the best and brightest of the Warsaw Pact).

In August 1993, SNA bombs began targeting US personnel. This action prompted the deployment of Task Force Ranger (TFR) under the command of Major General William Garrison. Garrison was a very well-respected soldier and TFR was afforded the best units and most advanced hardware from the entire US arsenal. This was intended to bring the manhunt for Aidid to a swift conclusion.

On 3 October 1993, actionable intelligence was received concerning a meet between two SNA militia and leaders from Aidid's Habar Gidir clan. Garrison duly deployed a capture force of 19 aircraft, 12 vehicles, and 160 soldiers. The 18-hour firefight ('the Battle of Mogadishu') cost the lives of 18 US soldiers and two UN peacekeepers, not to mention the 82 wounded and the loss of two MH-60 Black Hawks. Over 1,000 Somalis were killed during the battle.

What follows are five lessons from that action (this is not exhaustive) that should be considered within everyone's resilience planning and verification, be that military or commercial in nature:

1. **Perfect is the enemy of good:** Aidid was Western educated, led the overthrow of the last dictator, had children in the US, was sympathetic to US regional interests, and had previously offered to eliminate the Islamist militias (who later became al-

Shabaab) on behalf of the US. In short, he could have been a very powerful ally to further US interests in the region.

2. **Actions have consequences:** Conflicts have second- and third-order effects. Al-Qaeda later drew the US into Afghanistan after learning '...the Americans were not defeated militarily in Somalia... it fears being bogged down in a real war.' The Al-Qaeda/Aidid strategy link is more than simply compelling; rather, it is very close to being conclusive.
3. **Manage messaging:** Although the US won the battle, Aidid won the war. This was due to the psychology of a nation that recalled its deep scars from Vietnam and, even though a mortal blow had been dealt to the current enemy, it saw withdrawal as preferable to any further immediate loss of precious US life.
4. **Urban battles are fought on human terrain:** The protection offered by a 'local' population has the capacity to defeat almost any number of satellites or elite troops. In this instance, US intelligence struggled to function and was completely unaware of Aidid's location for the majority of its time in the region.
5. **Technology does not guarantee success:** The technology and personnel the US had at its fingertips were cutting edge. The team searching for Pablo Escobar was even reassigned to find Aidid. However, all this was ineffective against couriers and low-power walkie-talkies.

A few days after the battle, a mortar strike killed a US soldier and another 12 were injured. Even with Somali losses in the thousands and the momentum with the US, the sentiment in America turned and the public wanted their sons and daughters home. Civil war subsequently continued, and Aidid operated successfully in the region for another three years until he was shot in July 1996.

There is obviously far more to explore on this topic, and I have literally just scratched the surface. For example:

- The strategic trade-off between short-term losses and long-term costs is of interest.
- The tactical impact of the loss of a Black Hawk shot down by RPG the week before.
- Did this outcome result in the proliferation of pirate gangs in the region?
- How significant was the use of a remotely detonated antitank mine that was used to provoke the US in terms of the future use of improvised explosive devices (IEDs) in Iraq and Afghanistan?

There were also many nuances that even Ridley Scott avoided, perhaps because he thought them too farfetched. For instance, Aidid's son being a US Marine reservist, or that a CIA informant failed to give Aidid a gift with a concealed homing chip hidden inside because he lost a game of Russian roulette.

However, the biggest lesson for me was the role the American public was allowed to play. Aidid knew he was not a military match for Garrison, so he superseded that advantage by taking the battle to a different level and involving the American people by ensuring pictures of their dead soldiers were beamed directly into their homes. This elevated the conflict to a political level, and that was where he won against Garrison.

In short, by stirring painful memories (Vietnam), Aidid won the war and was arguably responsible for the future US absence on the world stage when the atrocities in Bosnia and genocide in Rwanda were addressed. If this case study teaches anything, it is not to discount the lesser of two evils, as it's often better the devil you know than to face the one you do not. Lastly, never forget to manage your key stakeholders (in this case, the American public dictated the outcome of this conflict from their sofas thousands of miles away).

In conclusion to this chapter, competent crisis management and emergency response is not the same as business management, and we must be careful not to base our planning on the flawed assumption of organisational theory that there is predictability in our world. In short, it is highly unlikely that any plan will survive first contact with the enemy, so we must rely on our people to direct operations to a safe conclusion, whilst not forgetting that there are tier one and tier two interested parties who must also be managed (in terms of both messaging and support).

Chapter Six

Training, Competence & Learning

'For the best return on your money, pour your purse into your head.'

—Benjamin Franklin

When I left university, I was recruited by a group of specialists who were at the top of their game (and still are, from what I hear). The defining factor of that time in my career was the inclusion of a mentor, who managed to forge my student mentality whilst feeding his own unique sense of humour by pointing me in the right direction, taking my leash off and then waiting for my youthful exuberance to reach its inevitable conclusion... stumble and fall (usually face down).

Self-preservation soon kicked in and Darwinian instincts made me recognise that my mentor was my shortest route to an easier life, because I did not like failing – and the team only had a limited tolerance for that type of failure. Back then, the world was not such a connected place and so my sources for progression were limited to those I worked with, along with the odd book. It was certainly a simpler world, and I enjoyed immersing myself in it.

I had no expectations for my day-to-day duties beyond being grateful for working with this group. I understood that it was a marathon in terms of my progression and the work was engaging, with lots of new opportunities involving challenge and stimulation. There was no social media to distort my reality and so I put my head down and learnt as much as I possibly could.

I never considered it was my right to be heard; I understood that I had to earn my voice. I did not take offence at someone who disagreed with me; I respected their opinion. I would never openly voice frustration at proven techniques or practices; I was trained to suggest and develop alternatives. I would never disagree with a client; I would manage my stakeholders.

We certainly joked by comparing ourselves to our Hollywood heroes, but this did not include being shamed into feelings of inadequacy after a hard day's work by the fictitiously perfect lives of social media influencers. The influencers back then were generally found in a pub, where their false claims were very publicly unearthed in a fun social (and often very unforgiving) setting.

One time in life was not better than another, but the influences have certainly changed. It would be a needless shame if there were those within your control who were unnecessarily suffering because you managed them in a similar style to the way you were managed, ultimately because you have failed to appreciate the degree to which the world has changed ('I had to do it that way and so must they').

The point of this story is to highlight that a mentor no longer has the influence they once did, and if we think they do then we are kidding ourselves. We need to appreciate that the world is so much more complex for our mentees; and, in the same way as my mentor(s) asked about my family and friends, we would do well to also consider social network influences.

Some would say (me included) that the ability to build a bond of trust with a mentee is the foundation of what separates the good mentors from the great. It should go without saying that enhancing an individual's technical know-how will invariably enable them to effectively leverage their place in the workplace hierarchy; however, true self-actualisation will be hard to come by if that is the total extent of the succession journey.

Over the years, I have found that the most important step on that road is the creation of a mutually agreed development plan that demonstrates to the mentee where they are, where they are going, what they need to do, and how progress can be measured. This methodology clarifies expectations and ensures that all parties involved create the levels of ownership and engagement necessary for the most effective experience possible.

It is also through such a plan that the mentor can assist the mentee to autonomously develop their own competence by nurturing their ability to self-correct. This ensures that each failure (a natural part of any development journey) is paired with a reflection that begins with 'What I should have done was...' Effectively, at this stage, the 'training wheels' are removed and the relationship turns from prescriptive to directional.

Of course, there is much more to write on this subject. Topics that spring to mind are the importance of an honest, two-way constructive dialogue that avoids false praise, a deep and meaningful appreciation and acceptance that everyone is different, that learning is not linear, the importance of understanding the whole person (and not just the professional) and many more. However, if I were to place one above the rest, it would be do not forget and/or underestimate the importance of a very simple and always accessible (referenceable as and when required) development plan.

If we turn our attention from mentoring to the process of learning, then I would like to start with a personal story that begins over two decades ago and is set in a normal-looking, large, white house in a nondescript rural road within a sleepy village in the northeast of England. What was unusual about this house was that the inside had been converted into the training wing of a very discreet organisation.

In the basement of that house, a lion of an operator, referred to as 'Dave', taught the art of close quarter battle (CQB) to the lucky ones who had made it that far in the organisation's selection process. For those not familiar, there are many elements to CQB, but it can be summarised as the use of well-planned and ultra-violent actions that are deployed to overcome an enemy, who is in close vicinity (<100m), by an unstoppably brutal physical and psychological momentum involving explosive speed, shocking aggression, and complete and total surprise.

On this day, the class were engaged in hand-to-hand training that was appropriate for high threat (anti-terrorist) protective duties. The specific scenario involved teams of students breaching rooms to overpower an unknown number of assailants that were armed with anything from rubber guns and decommissioned Uzi submachine guns to baseball bats and plastic knives.

Dave stewarded the group by gleefully 'beasting' us beyond our mental and physical capability and into a state of complete exhaustion. He did this because he knew that, in this space, he could programme our individual and collective muscle memory. I know this sounds harsh, but we were a robust group that had complete trust in our instructor, and my memories are of determination, smiles, and tears of laughter, whilst sweat poured into my eyes and the smell of rubber filled my nostrils from the array of gas masks we always had to wear.

One of the incredibly valuable aspects of Dave's training methods was to give us an insight into the stark reality of three scenarios: what we thought we could do (always wrong), what Dave knew we could do (always right), and the outcome if we pushed the boundaries beyond Dave's training (inevitable failure). By doing this, he instilled several life-saving values that stuck with us all through thick and thin. These were all based around the fact that the team works and to always trust your training.

Dave was unquestionably the very best at what he did. His genius in teaching was to stretch his pupils in the relentless pursuit of excellence, but to caveat that by occasionally tipping us over the edge into failure. It was only by showing us the balance of success against failure that we learnt to make informed decisions about our realistic capabilities. This meant that, when we planned, we did so with ultimate clarity on exactly how to achieve an objective. Ultimately, Dave's teachings saved lives.

We all like to train our personnel to succeed by showing them success. But, we would also do well to remember Dave's example and let our students experience (supported) failure to allow them to come to terms with the reality of a negative outcome. If we do not, we may be setting them up for real-world (unsupported and possibly terminal) failure by denying them half the story.

The fact that Western society subscribes to the concept that failure is intrinsically linked to a loss is strange to me and those with my background. My premise being, especially considering Dave, failure (a learning) cannot be a negative experience when it is an essential step to victory.

So, perhaps we would do better if we stopped assigning so much meaning to single events and outcomes and focus more on the journey. Thomas Edison famously said, 'I have not failed. I have just found 10,000 ways that will not work.' In short, persistence will nearly always beat resistance.

History teaches that it is rare to create something of real value on our first attempt. On a path less travelled, there is always a danger of ambush by unknown variables beyond our control. So, why not remove the self-inflicted pressure of a fixed outcome and break the connection between failure and a lack of self-worth? Not only are fixed outcomes aspirational (with reality rarely matching expectation), but they limit enjoyment, innovation, experience, etc.

In short, accepting failure relieves the unrealistic expectations of perfection. Not only will accepting that your endeavours are unlikely to be right first time release pressure, but it can be empowering! If we do not adopt that perspective, then we run the risk of self-sabotage. So, when someone says failure is not an option – they might be right, but it is nearly always a prerequisite to at least get to that point.

A critical aspect often neglected within the failure conversation is the role played by the job, individual and organisational factors, known as performance influencing factors (PIFs). PIFs can be single factors (or combinations thereof) that have potential to turn vulnerability into failure; and so, they could also be viewed, conversely, as criteria that we can actively manage to ensure that the risk of human failure is kept tolerable. PIFs can include, but are not limited to:

- **Job:** clarity of instructions; difficulty/complexity; routine/unusual; divided attention; procedures inadequate/inappropriate; time available versus required, etc.
- **Individual:** physical capability; fatigue (acute or chronic); stress/morale; work overload/underload; competence; motivation versus other priorities, etc.
- **Organisation:** production versus safety; supervision/leadership; communication; peer pressure; roles and responsibilities; organisational learning; culture, etc.

There are many methodologies that we can use to help us identify and manage PIFs. These range from crew resource management techniques (lists and aid memoires) to heat maps, which highlight the PIF combinations that hold elevated risk (and, of course, opportunity). To effectively manage PIFs, we need to educate the workforce on performance and safety essentials (generally one in the same). A large part of this task is to ensure that there is a correct pairing of required technical skills with their associated non-technical skills (NTS).

If we think of technical skills as the knowledge required to understand 'what' to do, NTS are the comprehension of 'how' to do it error-free. Therefore, NTS are critical in high-risk/high-reliability industries that rely on a human-machine/human-human interface in complex work environments. NTS can be subdivided into three categories: social, cognitive, and personal:

- **Social:** risk-based consideration of teamwork, leadership, communication.
- **Cognitive:** situation awareness, decision-making, readiness, and task management.
- **Personal:** suitable and sufficient assessment of stress and fatigue management.

So, if we are serious about error-proofing operations, particularly in high-risk and high-reliability industries (nuclear, aviation, oil and gas, etc.), then we must acknowledge and accept the role that PIFs and NTS play in achieving ALARP in error-likely environments. So, if your management system does not consider some or all the PIFs listed above, and make direct mention of the NTS, then you have an issue (that is exponentially higher if you work in an industry containing major accident hazards).

In terms of the importance of organisational learning, let us consider the Bradford City stadium fire that occurred on Saturday, 11 May 1985 at the Valley Parade Stadium. At 1540hrs, a television commentator spotted smoke, and less than four minutes later fire had engulfed the whole stand. Tragically, 56 of the 11,076 people in the ground lost their lives. Of that number: three had tried to escape through the toilets, 27 were found by exits and/or turnstiles (most of which had been locked), and two elderly persons died in their seats. Half of those who never made it home were aged under 20 or over 70 years old.

The fire is thought to have started when a cigarette was dropped through a floorboard and ignited the refuse under the seating. This was incredibly disappointing when it is considered that a letter from the local council in July 1984 warned that, 'A carelessly discarded cigarette could give rise to a fire risk.' This was because the main stand (seated 5,300) remained unaltered since its construction in 1886, and was made primarily of wood, with a roof covered with layers of highly flammable bituminous felt. It soon came to light that the stand had been condemned and was due to be replaced with a steel structure after the season ended.

The actual fire was first spotted by a witness who claims they saw debris alight about nine inches under the floorboards. Due to the seats not having risers, a relatively large accumulation of waste was in the cavity under the structure. This mix propagated a fierce blaze that spread with ease and the police quickly began to evacuate the stand. There were no extinguishers in the stand's passageway for fear of vandalism, and so it took less than four minutes for the entire stand to be engulfed in flames. Those in the stand either ran to the back of the stand (where most of the exits were locked or shut) or down onto the pitch to escape.

In the end, the Bradford City stadium fire was the result of a catalogue of errors and missed warnings. Those same warnings could have prevented another disaster. In the aftermath of the Bradford fire, it was pointed out that many of the supporters had escaped the flames by climbing out of the stands and onto the pitch. However, due to the focus on the rolc played by the combustible nature of wooden stands, little attention was paid to the difficulty of evacuating supporters. Four years later, on 15 April 1989, Liverpool played Nottingham Forest at Hillsborough in the FA Cup. On that day, 96 people were crushed to death, unable to escape onto the pitch because of the high fences. The 97th victim has now died, yet another needless loss because of a lack of organisational learning.

With failure and organisational learning in mind, we owe a lot to Hermann Ebbinghaus (German psychologist) for pioneering early work on memory and attempting to plot the rate of information retention versus time, known as the Forgetting Curve. Ebbinghaus' work concluded that 42% of information was lost after 20 minutes, 56% was gone after an hour, 64% could not be recalled after 9 hours, and nearly 80% had been forgotten after a month.

I feel compelled to point out that Ebbinghaus' work did not contain the reliability and/or validity required for us to confidently generalise it to the wider population. However, Ebbinghaus did prove that we are all subject to an alarmingly high rate of memory attrition concerning training content. What we can also conclude from his work is that the 'curve' would, most likely, be different for everyone.

So, now that we know that there is a steep curve to information retention and attrition, we are morally and legally obliged to turn the focus on ourselves. For example, under the UK's duty of care legal principal, employers have a general duty to employees to provide 'information, instruction, training and supervision' so that risks can be suitably managed whilst work is completed.

The question we must ask ourselves is, how we (the employers) are achieving that duty when evidence suggests over half of the training content that we assign to our personnel is lost after an hour. This surely means that we cannot realistically hold someone accountable for performing a non-compliant action, when the original instruction was received via a 15-second snippet of information buried in an hour-long computer-based course that was completed over a year ago.

This means that training can be a black art to the uninitiated and, without an immediate and measurable key performance indictor (KPI) showing a return on investment (ROI), it can be problematic to build a compelling business case to senior management.

Perhaps it is an overdue exercise for us all to consider just how effective our organisation's current training is, how vulnerable our operational risk profiles are to the forgetting curve, and what we can do to maximise information retention, whilst ensuring attrition is confined to non-critical paths.

David Kolb (educational theorist) released a model in 1984 based on experiential learning that can help. The Learning Styles and Experiential Learning Cycle evaluates the learning experience, and then uses the outcome to tailor individualistic employee learning strategies.

The process begins by having a competent trainer run an employee through a four-stage methodology, which identifies the learning style(s) that best suits the individual in question. This generally results in a blended approach, whilst also highlighting styles that do not suit the individual's specific learning needs (very important).

These insights can then be applied to an experiential learning cycle to map a bespoke Learning Style Inventory (LSI), which is effectively a person's 'learning DNA'. This can then be given to a trainer in advance of them delivering a course, to ensure that the content and format are suitably tailored to optimise the individual's learning experience.

This highlights that information attrition must be factored into any meaningful training (especially safety critical) if it is delivered in a broad-brush format to a room of unique professionals (all of which have their own optimal learning style). It also reinforces understanding that an employee's learning style is a precondition to any training value creation.

In terms of self-value creation, many managers and leaders follow the five-hour rule (whether they realise it or not). This was born from Ben Franklin's belief in never-ending self-development. To facilitate the process, he reserved five hours a week for self-improvement. This meant he began each working day by reading for an hour, followed by time reflecting on the text, then embarking on his day whilst looking for ways to apply relevant aspects of what he had read.

While most people generally appear intrigued when they first hear of this technique, some feel compelled to validate themselves by claiming they don't have five spare hours a week in their diary. My answer to that is self-improvement is not a 'spare' activity, it is fundamental to your very core. People then usually agree it is not a time issue, but a failure to prioritise what is important.

It is a surprise to most when they learn that Barack Obama credits the five-hour rule with surviving his presidency. Gates, Musk, Oprah, and Buffett also attribute their successes (in part) to the rule. Interestingly, although application has obviously changed since Franklin's time, there are three constants to which all successful advocates stay true: read, reflect and experiment:

- **Read:** In terms of the availability of information, we are fortunate to live in the time we do. Online journals, webinars, research papers and/or (good old) print are available to almost all of us. Personally, I bookmark my favourite sources and spend 15 minutes in the morning (with a coffee) and a further 15 minutes in the afternoon (with a decaf) scrolling through them.
- **Reflect:** The difference between the person I am today, and the student that I once was, is the realisation that learning has nothing to do with memorising information, and everything to

do with the interpretation of meaning. For that reason, I add another five minutes to each 15 minutes of reading so that I can reflect, digest, and truly understand the content.

- **Experiment:** This is a key principle in learning and development, and ultimately woven into our DNA as a species. Not only is this intensely interesting, but it is only by the application of ideas that we can truly declare that something 'works'. However, caution must be exercised, as experimentation (by its nature) means that we must stretch beyond the 'known' status quo.

...and then there is my own addition to Franklin's rule, and where my articles come from...

- **Sharing:** This takes up the remaining 20 minutes a day and is both cathartic and rewarding. In my experience, there are many within the world of work (particularly in early career stages) that confuse becoming better at their work as self-improvement. By falling into this trap, we risk developing an imbalance between personal and professional characters, which can result in someone who is great in the office but lost outside it (a depressingly common outcome).

When we talk about making a change for the better, a New Year's resolution would be a good place to start. There have been years when I have been adamant that 1 January would herald a new beginning; and, the next year, I am puzzled as to why I would wait for a specific date to make a change. I am glad to say that this paradox does not only affect me.

Reassuringly, American research reveals that it is common to break life into chapters, often defined by major life events. This explains why we reflect on 'the old me' and provides a helpful 'fresh start' when required. So, if we use the New Year as our own 'fresh start', what type of resolutions would give us the best chance of success?

Research from Stockholm University found that there is an advantage to classifying a resolution into either 'avoidance' or 'approach' objectives. Avoidance goals would result in purposely omitting something from life (such as sugar); whereas, approach goals would involve adding something into one of life's routines (such as exercise). The research found we are 25% more likely to meet an approach goal than an avoidance one.

Data also tells us that about a quarter of people make at least one New Year's resolution. Of that, about 35% manage to complete them successfully, with another 50% keeping to 'some of them'. This means that New Year adds more value to our lives than we might have realised.

What we do know is that the road to self-improvement is rarely easy. If you are on that journey (which I hope this book is helping with), why not make approach goals rather than avoidance goals? It may also help to divide your goals into periods of time so that you can give yourself some fresh starts along the way.

The pandemic caused the world's commercial graveyards to quickly fill with those companies that realised too late that their pandemic survivability was dictated by their own scalability. A continually growing list of company casualties has proven this beyond any reasonable doubt, and the axiom that has emerged is that the modern world belongs to those who embrace changing market conditions.

The oil and gas industry has long since recognised the benefits of such agility, not always as the result of insightful acumen, but usually due to the battle scars of conducting legacy business within such a volatile boom-and-bust market. The industry has subsequently learnt to plan by risk profile (the balance of capacity/tolerance/requirement), which gives a journey map to organisational technical limits.

Each technical limit relies upon a huge number of variables, but primarily the foundations are rooted within the building blocks of operational integrity (people/plant/process). Ironically, what I see most commonly are disproportionate amounts of resources spent on equipment assurance and management system verification, with little attention devoted to the greatest potential for ROI, the people.

In most organizations and in almost every sector, survival in today's commercial world depends upon creating the capacity and capability within the workforce to learn faster than competitors. This can create a defining competitive advantage. With that in mind, set in a backdrop of tight cost control, it is still common to find organization's haemorrhaging cost with expensive staff training programmes that have little-to-no bearing on the company ability to achieve its strategic objectives.

This is not a surprise when we consider $359billion is spent on training globally; but 70% of employees don't feel they have the skills needed for their jobs, and only 12% say they have ever applied what was learned from company training. One of the potential answers is...

Lean learning offers something different, and creates a focus on identifying core skills, applying them to real-world scenarios and then receiving feedback which is then used to immediately refine understanding...and then the cycle is repeated. This technique pays homage to Toyota's lean manufacturing, it stresses effort only when needed, improving outcomes, and cutting waste; it's short, affordable, and provides employees and organizations with an immediate capability update.

This must link learning to business outcomes, meaning the organisation must alter it's their view on the purpose of training from compliance and performance, and transfer ownership from an HR function to employee and line management. We then test that we are teaching the right things, at the right time, for the right reasons by analysing the only metric that really counts, achieving the strategy.

If this chapter has made you question the effectiveness of your company's training then reverse engineer your organization's strategic success criteria and apply the Pareto Principle (80/20). What you are left with is a learning quota with a high return on investment. If that does not loosely resemble what you are offering your workforce, then you might have a problem (or even an opportunity).

In conclusion to this chapter, learning to fail is one of the most pivotal lessons that any professional can make, and must be supported within the working environment. It is essential that we recognise that we are all different learners, and that we naturally forget information over time, as well as have a duty to continue to learn to reach our potential. Lastly, true development involves the whole person, and transcends far beyond simple technical skills.

Chapter Seven

Branding, Marketing, Storytelling & Information.

'If you don't give the market the story to talk about,

they'll define your brand's story for you.'

—David Brier

The rate of specialists being promoted to business generalists without succession planning or developmental training is growing by the day. This is leading to a generation of managers who have been promoted based on their success in previous jobs, until they reach a level at which they are no longer competent. This is generally known as the Peter Principle, which highlights to us that skills in one job do not necessarily translate into competence within another role.

With that in mind, I thought it may add value to outline the fundamental difference between three concepts that are considered confusing dark arts by most graduates of the Peter Principle. Those concepts are branding, marketing, and sales.

Branding shapes the market's impression (includes customer experience) and is a driver to loyalty. This contrasts with marketing, which encompasses promotional activities to create the leads that the sales team turns into customers. The three separate functions all contain distinct processes and specialist roles that work in harmony to drive value creation. They are linked, but they are definitely not the same.

When you build an identity (brand), the focus is on the image that you want to portray, which is not the same as engaging an audience (marketing). There are also differences in duration, with branding strategies requiring longer-term careful management, in contrast to fast-paced marketing campaigns which require agile thinking and a deep understanding of the target demographic.

As for the interface dynamic, strong branding is best informed by good marketing, and good marketing is driven by strong branding. In terms of workforce branding, a Brandfrog study (2016) found that 75% of those questioned thought that the nature of an employee's social media presence made a brand more trustworthy, with 68% believing that a CEO without a web-based presence would be disregarded as irrelevant.

This type of market chatter is now appearing in tidal proportions, and takes branding strategy beyond the 'page spread in an industry journal' to the engagement of all employees in flying the virtual branding flag. This consideration should also stretch far beyond digital platforms, to include any interaction where professionals can create and share quality content that feeds a branding picture.

With that in mind, marketing is something that is best left to the discipline-specific professionals. However, as any marketing expert will also testify, helping key personnel construct their own professional brand (that complements stakeholders), and then encouraging them to intelligently drive quality content on multiple platforms, is now a requirement, and not a choice, for effective strategy.

This means I would suggest you think again if you banish social media (LinkedIn, Twitter, etc.) to a 'lunch-hour activity', or scoff at a motivated team member who asks for (unproductive) time out of the office and a budget to attend forums. The market is telling us, in no uncertain terms, that you should in fact be doing the opposite and embracing these activities (and many more non-traditional avenues) as core competencies within a managed strategy to deliver an honest and consistent message to the market.

At this point, it would be valuable to address storytelling, which is a key tool in the branding toolbox. Organisational psychologists have long since recognised the benefits of storytelling in terms of visual, auditory, and even kinesthetics learning, with some research suggesting a 20x improvement in information retention. With such an obvious vehicle to engagement and inspiration, safety moments can be used as a good example of powerful messaging tools (but the same concept can be used for leadership, sales, etc.). Here are four tips regarding a safety moment's delivery:

1. They are what their name suggests, a 'moment'. These sound bites should not be onerous, as their purpose is to frame the meeting topic. To do this competently should take no more than three or four minutes.
2. They have relevance that resonates with the audience. I would not expect a meeting that is attended by globally revered subject

matter experts to begin with an engineer waxing lyrical about home DIY.

3. They are not interactive sessions. Each moment should deliver a clear message within an interesting and relevant context. This is not to say that questions/comments should not be invited, just that this is not the time for debate.
4. They are not delivered by those with senior management titles. The workforce contains an incredibly impressive diversity of thought, perspective, and experience. A safety moment is an excellent opportunity to access that rich resource.

A safety moment is certainly not required in all meetings; a values moment, instead, to highlight the 'right' priorities might work better within other (financial or HR) settings. However, if the chosen moment (whatever its content and/or intent) does not survive the substitution test, then please think again. You might well be wasting an incredibly valuable opportunity to persuade a certain type of thinking.

It would be a struggle to find a respected leader anywhere in the world who would deny that 'persuasion' plays a pivotal role in leadership. This is critically reinforced by credibility, which is linked to their professional branding. It would be difficult to exert influence if you were known to be self-serving, weak, or immoral.

However, most corporate leaders are held back due to their own struggle to deliver compelling encouragement. This is not always their fault, with most organisations omitting leadership training from their succession planning. This results in senior leaders who rarely stray from a series of predictable PowerPoint and email templates that have been heavily filtered (if not written) by a corporate communication function.

What this has essentially created, is a level of hierarchy that has lost the ability to tell stories. The reason is that corporate leaders tend to rely on an intellectual connection (level one) made with a business case supported by vanilla rhetoric (statistics and facts). However, can we say that, from our experience, people are inspired by intellectual connection? I don't know about you, but I know that I certainly need more than that.

Have you ever been to a conference where someone takes to the stage and captivates the audience? I am willing to bet they did not do it with a PowerPoint slide pack full of statistics. That is where storytelling creates an emotional attachment (level two), to work in tandem with the intellectual connection and elevate the storyteller (hopefully) from good to great.

The good news is that the fundamentals of a story have remained constant. It begins with a benign scene within which there is an 'event'. This twist is powerful enough to change the direction of the story toward the unexpected. The protagonist must overcome a challenge to reset the chain of events back to the original path... and everyone lives happily ever after.

So, whether it is a future vision or recalling events from the past that define your values, try telling a strategic story. It is not difficult, just a simple piece of prose which offers little more than a vivid insight into how and why a change happens. Not only will your workforce thank you, but your business will, too.

A great example of this is a story that has driven many recruits across the threshold of the US Army Rangers. The notorious and infamous event happened in America in the 1980s. At that time, the country was (in)famous for many things, not all of which were featured in the clean-cut movies that I remember from my childhood. One aspect that everyone would like to forget was the overnight explosion in drugs, driven by the severe economic downturn.

The drug gangs were indiscriminate and spread like parasites; they infested virgin territory and left nothing behind but pain, devastation, and broken communities. Tacoma, Washington, was a very typical example of a community that was subjected to an uncontrolled influx of gang activity.

The gangs appeared with such pace that law enforcement was left outgunned and out resourced. In Tacoma, one of the leaders of the local drug gang (associated with 'The Crips') lived on Ash Street and was responsible for turning that neighbourhood into an open-air and very public drugs bazaar.

On 23 September 1989, a quiet and unassuming man, who also lived on Ash Street, approached the gang leader and asked him to stop his activity and change his ways. The man was told to leave by the gang leader, and his life threatened. Later that day, the gang destroyed the CCTV at the man's home. This led the man to believe the gang intended to carry out their threats at his house later that day.

The man (who was Second Ranger Battalion Staff Sgt. William Foulks) asked his wife to leave the property and then invited over some friends for a BBQ. A short time later, 10 to 15 serving Rangers arrived with their personal firearms and an uncommonly large amount of ammunition for a BBQ. The party got underway, but was stopped when a shot in the general direction of the house rang out just after dusk. The soldiers took defensive positions around the property.

Just after 9 pm, more shots were heard, and this time the Rangers returned fire. The one-sided firefight lasted for 10 minutes before local police arrived (to the relief of the gang members). At this point, the Rangers ceased fire and surrendered their weapons. The Rangers had been careful not to use lethal force, but had sent a very effective message that purposely did not involve blood, this time.

The police did not arrest any of the Rangers and the official response from their commanding officer was that his troops had acted in 'self-defence' during a private party. The Ash Street shootout was a turning point in the fight back against the local drug gangs, and instrumental in transforming that neighbourhood into one of the safest in the city. Rumour has it that Staff Sgt. William Foulks still lives there!

However, when telling these stories and interfacing with the market, we must make sure that our message is clear and understood. This was not done in the case of A&W Restaurants, an American chain of fast-food restaurants that are famous for two things: the first being their 'frosty mugs' (kept in a freezer and filled with root beer just before serving), the second being an ability to make delicious burgers.

In the 1980s, A&W squared off against McDonald's with a burger that had more meat (1/3 pound), performed better in blind taste tests than the McDonald's alternative (1/4 pounder), and sold at a lower price. With all these attributes, A&W were predicting a landslide win.

What happened was a magnificent flop. Alfred Taubman, the owner of A&W at the time, immediately launched an investigation and employed the famous social scientist Daniel Yankelovich to help his team of in-house hamburger experts discover the reason for the failure.

Yankelovich immediately formed a focus group that quickly identified negative pricing sentiment because, 'Why should we pay the same amount for a third of a pound of meat as we do a quarter pound of meat at McDonald's? You are overcharging us.'

It became apparent that the tastier and bigger burger was lagging behind its more expensive and smaller competitor because of a belief that a third of a pound was less than a quarter of a pound (three is less than four). The lesson is that the customer is king, and message and signposting needs to be crystal clear.

Another example was during the pandemic, when people naturally scrambled for threat data and often turned to online sources. Reuters Institute for the Study of Journalism found that news-related searches immediately spiked with traffic to the likes of the BBC News website, more than doubling in March 2020.

This led to social media quickly establishing itself as a perceived source of 'valid' data. In the UK alone, there was a 9% increase in the use of social media for news by the under 35s from January and April 2020. Smaller increases were also observed within all other demographics.

This rapid growth provided the perfect opportunity for disinformation, which fuelled a hungry media and resulted in occasions of violent public reactions. An example of this being arson attacks on communications infrastructure due to the belief that COVID-19 linked to 5G.

We know now that the murky world of social media platforms act as information gatekeepers, a fact made prominent by Brexit and the Trump presidential election. The evidence of coordinated malicious influence in both of those scenarios is now undeniable.

In 2020, we saw another evolution in consumption and moderation of social media output. This triggered the platforms, that had been traditionally reluctant to implement any censorship, enter unprecedented relationships with various governments and other entities.

For example, Google prioritises World Health Organisation results, with Twitter and Facebook both having algorithms displaying links to regionally appropriate authorities in newsfeeds. These steps depart from the 'arbiter of truth' role previously claimed by all three.

What the COVID-19 pandemic effectively did was demonstrate that freedom of speech against regulation/moderation can be overridden when there is a clear and credible threat to public safety. This should not be forgotten when the current crisis subsides, and the next inevitably approaches.

However, harmful content does not always originate from malicious actors. It can be from an information demand that outstrips supply, which draws in partial research and unproven results to a politically charged debate; this, in turn, legitimises multiple interpretations of threat.

We have learnt that communication must be proactive, safe and secure, simple, and accessible to an audience. It must acknowledge uncertainty, and be capable of performing in a social media context (of note: even 'memes' have proven very successful in gaining viral visibility).

The use of TikTok by the Red Cross to spread vital messaging also shows us that the medium must be relevant and catchy. What is certain is that post-pandemic communications are a far cry from those of the pre-pandemic days, given what we now know.

The inconvenient truth is that we are all programmed to believe what we read. This trait has been fostered over generations by well-meaning parents who began to shape young minds through the pages of storybooks; a heuristic developed by religious leaders who deliver sermons involving 'faith' and a 'good book'. These teachings are then reinforced by educators, who encourage us to memorise textbooks in a programme of positive reinforcement.

It is hard to deny that we are nurtured to believe what we read first, and then question as an afterthought. This ingrained behavioural set is then exposed to a corporately sponsored world communicated through an unregulated internet, to give rise to the modern digital misinformation landscape.

This new data-filled environment, typified by cutting-edge technology under a 'click-bait' philosophy, has meant the collapse of the traditional information gatekeeper model. As a result of the crumbling of those time-tested barriers, there is a growing number of examples showcasing the dangers of an information-illiterate society.

One such example would be that of Cambridge Analytica, where a seemingly harmless Facebook quiz mined the data of 87 million users. This information was then used to create targeted campaigns for the 2016 Trump presidential effort, an election that is said to have been won and lost by 'fake' Twitter accounts that undermined the integrity of the Obama administration.

This was all made possible because humans have an inbuilt bias that is employed to align the information we receive with our existing beliefs. Therefore, it is easier to convince a person that something is true when it supports what they already believe. This process is known as motivated reasoning.

In contrast, we need plenty of evidence that is delivered in the right way to convince us that something outside of our existing belief system is correct. Social media has proven this, with users quickly sharing political articles that support their views, but fact checking all others.

Conflict often arises when moral and factual judgements are confused (when the 'right' thing is not backed by data). This leads to those who strongly identify with a concept feeling increasingly frustrated that all others are seemingly ignoring the blatantly obvious.

These issues are compounded by an online world that provides unlimited opportunities to 'cherry pick'. This kind of echo chamber gives the freedom to choose a preferred reality and is a common outcome of 'retained opinion'. This is when false information is released and, even when categorically proven as a lie, continues to influence.

For example, Stanford University (2015) told a group of students that firefighters were risk averse and told another group the opposite. All students were then told the information was false. A short time later, they were asked about the traits of a firefighter, and everyone aligned with what they had been originally told. This demonstrates that lies have a legacy, and we need to rethink how we qualify data (the backbone of media literacy).

This was shown (again) in the pandemic, when the data said the vaccine was effectively a 'no brainer' for most, but many remained overtly sceptical and, in some cases, irrational. One reason was that certain media establishments used the base rate fallacy to their gain, something increasingly common within unregulated social media.

This is when a critical contextual characteristic is purposely omitted to ensure data can only be considered in silo, rather than with due consideration of all sources. Imagine a social media post that stated 40% of new COVID-19 infections were in those who were vaccinated. At first glance, that would make us question the efficacy of a vaccine.

However, within that questioning we would establish base rate consideration(s), which would inform our decision-making. In this example, the population had an 80% vaccine rate, which meant that the remaining 20% accounted for 60% of new infections. Suddenly, getting a vaccine makes sense again.

I would like to end this chapter with a tragic example of the importance of effective communication. The Falklands conflict was a 74-day undeclared war between Argentina and the UK. During that time, a Royal Navy Type 42 destroyer mistakenly engaged a British Army Gazelle in a friendly fire incident, resulting in the death of all four personnel onboard.

The navy's destroyer was tasked with a dual mission, which involved providing fire support for the Royal Marines and searching for enemy aircraft. During the mission, a radar contact was made with what was thought to be a hostile target and so a Sea Dart missile was sent to intercept. The wreckage of the army's Gazelle helicopter was recovered the next day.

The subsequent investigation identified several factors that allowed the event to occur. Poor communication had meant a) the navy's destroyer was unaware of the army helicopter flight path, and b) the army helicopter was unaware that the navy destroyer had redeployed to ambush enemy aircraft. Also, the helicopter's friend/foe system was disabled to prevent interference with other military technology (specifically, Rapier surface-to-air missiles).

I would suggest that recounting this example within an operational environment, that involves multiple service providers, would be valuable. It would highlight the vital role of planning, communication, and the interface management of people/processes/technology. As a last note: after the conflict, a memorial cross was built on Pleasant Peak. A '205' was painted in 40-metre-wide numbers at the crash site by the soldiers of 205 Signal Squadron. I visited that site in 2016 to pay my respects.

In conclusion to this chapter, never underestimate the power of corporate storytelling in terms of branding and/or marketing. However, in the same vein, beware of informational influences from unverified sources. Unregulated information sources are regularly at the heart of poor decisions, conflict, and tragedy.

Chapter Eight

Culture, Performance and Rest

'To win in the marketplace you must first win in the workplace.'

–Douglas Conant

Steve Jobs typified the benefits of fusing values and performance to attract market share and talent. This strategy was one of the many catalysts he used to create one of the most successful companies of all time. This reinforces the point that values really are essential in achieving a vision and to define how an organisation conducts its mission. So, whilst workforce skills provide the critical capability, they can be replaced, but the same cannot be said about their values.

When hiring managers, an organisation must now choose between someone who can do what they want or selecting someone who wants what they want. The choice may not be binary, but when the rapid nature of technical advances and skills attrition are factored in, it makes sense to lean towards the latter.

What have not changed are the fundamentals within the art of leadership (see Chapter One). The function is not to plan and direct, but to inspire and empower. Leaders must remember that capabilities are critical to achieving their goals, but those capabilities are only made possible by people.

This means that a winning team is not necessarily a team full of winners. A winning team is a collective that prioritises long-term vision over short-term satisfaction. A group of people willing to help each other to advance, because it is unilaterally accepted that the best path is one which is travelled together.

Safety culture can also be thought of as the collective commitment from individual and shared values, perceptions, attitudes, competencies, and behavioural patterns. Predictably, when dealing with such a diverse mix, the output rarely sits uniformly throughout an organisation.

The variance is the natural result of the way the various internal and external influences are felt by the different individuals, teams, departments, and organisations. This subsequently creates a bumpy landscape that comprises multiple favourable and unfavourable pockets of culture.

This means that, without the mapping necessary to highlight the cultural peaks and troughs, a manager can only ever have a false economy of confidence in their team's performance.

The methodology used to clear the mists and provide such mapping is termed a 'climate' survey. This is because of the parallels that can be drawn between the fluctuations in a cultural landscape, and the changeable patterns on a meteorological map.

So, the question you must now be asking is what defines good and bad 'cultural' weather:

1. **Leadership:** This encompasses if safety is perceived to be as an organisational priority, and is generally shaped by how the company balances profitability against safety.
2. **Communication:** This involves effective dialogue throughout the hierarchy, particularly in terms of raising issues and then arriving at resolutions that satisfy all parties.
3. **Engagement:** A measure of structured involvement (representatives, workshops, etc.), as well as loss event reporting (real and potential) to foster continuous improvement.
4. **Training and information:** Creating a workforce with an accurate hazard perception, who can then make confident, informed decisions about risk appetite and tolerances.
5. **Motivation:** This involves the pride felt by the workforce and integrates the harmony between workforce/management expectations, particularly for reward and discipline.
6. **Governance:** Compliance with a risk-based management system that contains accurate and realistic work instructions within a work environment that is set up for success.
7. **Learning:** Does the organisation learn from its own operations, as well as the context in which it operates (cross-industry), and is the workforce kept informed of this progress.

If done correctly, using climate surveys to measure safety culture gives a handsome return on investment. I have many clients who have elevated their values and culture to almost cult-like status and have subsequently enjoyed an enhanced company reputation and established management credibility, whilst simultaneously reducing loss and growing profit.

If we were to take the concept of a cult to an extreme level (but with lessons that could be somewhat adapted to the commercial environment), becoming a terrorist rarely involves a conscious decision and is far more likely to be due to a gradual exposure and socialisation to specific rhetoric. The onward paths between 'become' and 'remain' then lie within motive and vulnerability. We can think of motive as the incitement to action (often talked of as the 'cause'), whereas vulnerability would be the susceptibility to succumb. Vulnerability is incredibly complex and spans across all demographics in terms of injustice, identity and belonging:

- **Injustice:** Imagined or real injustice helps us understand violence in general. It involves the innate desire for revenge or vengeance to redress or remediate a wrong. This begins with a grievance which can be subdivided into economic, ethnic, racial, legal, political, religious and/or social against individuals, groups, institutions, or just specific categories of people.
- **Identity:** This can be thought of in terms of values, attitudes, and beliefs. This is commonly formed in adolescence/early adulthood crisis and involves emotionally challenging periods that leave the person feeling marginalised. This points the person towards collectives with ideologies that resonate with those overwhelmed by the complexity of a complicated world.

- **Belonging:** Many find a sense of meaning and gain the affiliation they have lacked in life whilst being otherwise alienated by society. Membership serves as a protective cocoon and offers the first real sense of belonging after prolonged periods of rejection, providing the security of an otherwise absent 'family'. This is critical in terms of joining/staying/acting.

We know the path to terrorism is different for all, but generally begins with an awareness of oppression, moves to the recognition that it is unavoidable, follows an impetus to act, then is immediately preceded by the realisation that conventional acts will fail. If those ingredients are mixed with an early life socialisation event, circumstances that affect self-esteem and then escalatory acts (maybe involving police, etc.), and there is an existing connection (physical or virtual) with a group, then they are vulnerable for recruitment.

Whilst we are not aiming towards making terrorists, there are lessons here to do with your company reputation, values, vision and mission, which are adaptable to creating a loyal and engaged workforce. It is also interesting to ensure an inclusive environment, and the impact left on the minority who do not 'belong'.

I recently saw the collateral damage of poorly managed engagement initiatives on two seasoned professionals that I hold in the highest regard, and who have now each been left in uncomfortable no-win scenarios:

- The first person, a conservative and well-spoken 60-year-old in London, recently explained to me over coffee how awkward he felt sharing the score on his company well-being app. He said that this was now encouraged to be a cultural norm in his organisation. For him, however, and a few others, this kind of transparency was against his nature and encroached on some of his life choices outside the office (personal aspects that have nothing to do with an employer).
- The second person was in Aberdeen, and he recalled being unofficially approached by human resources to suggest he swap one of his lunchtime walks with an 'activity class' in the company gym. This is a proud man who has worn a shirt and tie to work for the past 40 years; the thought of entering the company gym whilst wearing shorts and a t-shirt genuinely distressed him.

Both were as bemused as they were bewildered when they told me their stories. But, when I asked if I could write about them in this book, they both admitted that it was a story they would like to be told. This is because they do not feel they can voice their feelings for fear of being labelled a 'dinosaur', and they both also recognise the good that such initiatives do for others.

The lesson here is that, as our workplace evolves, we must respect the fact that, as much as inclusion involves everyone, it does not mean forceful participation. Whilst some want a work family, others are not interested in 'opening up' while sitting on beanbags; instead, they feel more comfortable in a suit and tie with clear demarcation of personal and private. In short, some people just want a job, not a cult.

Speaking of records, if you thought athletic records were due to advances in physical prowess, then you would be wrong. Data tells us that the lion's share of advancement now comes from technology. For example, in 1972 the longest distance cycled in an hour was 30.5 miles, a figure that grew to 35 miles in 1996. However, when the riders used similar bikes, the 4.5 mile increase was reduced to only 270 metres.

There are several other examples of the value of technological evolution. It would not necessarily be a surprise to learn that Usain Bolt (fabricated track/angled blocks/wearing spikes) would likely finish 4.3 metres ahead of Jesse Owens (on cinders/starting holes dug with trowel/plimsolls). However, if those differentiators were removed, then the difference at the finish is thought to be only 1 metre.

This also correlates with the four-minute mile (1954), which was also run on cinders. In 2014, a total of 1,314 athletes ran the time. However, if the 1.5% performance enhancement (from cinders to synthetic track) was removed, the figure would drop to 513. This is a 60% false economy in perceived human performance.

We would be mistaken to think it is all technology; but genes also play their part. During the 1920s, the average elite high jumper and shot putter were the exact same size. Today, the difference is about 2.5 inches and 130 pounds. In America, if you meet a male between the ages of 20 and 40 who is over 7 feet tall, then there's a 1 in 6 chance that he's an NBA player.

Lastly, and my favourite, are the Kenyan runners from the Kalenjin tribe. A total of 32 men within that tribe ran marathons in under 2 hours 10 minutes in October 2014; that's nearly double the number of American men that have ever done the same.

Beyond the technology and genes, mindset is of critical importance. The world is full of examples of superhuman feats of performance, such as Kilian Jornet, who ran up and down the Matterhorn (8,000ft) in under three hours. This was made possible, in no small part, due to a mindset change from victory and towards consistent and constant improvement.

This exploration would not be complete without mention of the work of Anders Ericsson (1993). It was Ericsson who concluded that top-ranked violinists must clock up 10,000 hours of practice. It was from this hypothesis that the belief was born that you need to devote 10,000 hours to master a craft.

Even Ericsson's own hypothesis points us towards practice as the key that unlocks everything from 'sprinting to surgery'; but that, then, raises the question of how much practice hits the sweet-spot in a Goldilocks-type quandary (too much or too little are both destructive).

What is certain is that we would be mistaken to think that it is only the traditionally recognised factors that make average people excellent in their chosen arena. So, we can say that there is an equilibrium of excellence which balances technological, physical, and psychological elements.

We can identify similar traits within the 'makeup' of the majority of those we would popularly term 'top performers'. It is common to see aspects in their life that indirectly assist in helping them achieve the marginal gains that work to separate them from the pack. These can range from complementary hobbies to strategic relationships and can be interdependent.

What is a prerequisite of all, be it for Olympian or business titan, is achieving quality sleep. It is a fact that allowing your heart to rest and cells to repair promotes health and well-being, without which your cardiovascular health would suffer almost immediately.

When you are asleep, your body produces cytokines to help the immune system fight infections and assist in all forms of recovery. These restorative effects improve your mood, decrease the risk of developing physical and/or mental health illness and are the key to your resilience.

Sleep also helps you retain and consolidate the memories that are made during the process of learning. Without sleep, the neural pathways that allow recall cannot be effectively formed; this means that, if you are in a job that requires high cognitive function and/or are faced with rapidly changing circumstances, then your performance will be dramatically hindered.

One study found that competitive tennis players who increased their sleep to nine hours a night saw serve accuracy gains between 36% and 42%, whilst another group who suffered mild sleep deprivation saw accuracy fall by 53% when compared to normal performance.

It would be a mistake to think that too little sleep is the only hazard; the opposite is also true. The *Journal of the American Heart Association* published a meta-analysis of more than three million people and found those who slept over nine hours a day died earlier, with those sleeping 11 hours increasing their odds for an early demise by over 50%.

In general, most adults need between six to nine hours, with those in sports ranging between seven and nine hours. Elite athletes are now encouraged to aim for nine hours and treat rest as they would diet, as an essential. This, then, leads the conversation back to how much sleep is required by an 'office athlete' who is very cognitively active. On this, opinions vary, but I would warn that if you are sleeping less than six hours then you could be heading for issues, not least with your concentration.

There are several internal and external ways to prevent and mitigate burnout, but perhaps the most fundamental of them all is simply that of 'rest'. There is a common misconception that rest is another word for sleep; but, as anyone with experience of burnout will testify, no amount of sleep can reignite motivation or provide a path of escape from the overwhelming feeling of professional exhaustion.

The truth is that just because someone has had 'enough' sleep, it does not then mean they are rested to an extent that allows them to consistently perform at their potential. All of us have a duty to play our part in educating our own workforce to this fact, and therefore prevent the spread of a culture perpetuated by high-achieving, chronically tired and burnt-out professionals.

With that in mind, I would suggest that the following seven key areas of rest (or close iterations) should be deemed as essential within any continuous professional development programme:

- **Physical:** Although this can take the form of sleep (passive), physical rest can also include restorative activities that help improve circulation and flexibility (yoga).
- **Mental:** If you have difficulty concentrating/switching off from your day, then you may have a mental rest deficit. Try scheduling frequent short breaks during your day.
- **Sensory:** Things like being constantly 'connected' and open-plan offices can cause us to be overwhelmed. Intentional sensory deprivation can undo this type of damage.
- **Creative:** This is especially important for problem solvers and involves turning their working environment into an inspiration for innovation as opposed to a grey box.
- **Emotional:** This involves having the time and space to freely express your feelings and cut back on people pleasing, but critically involves the courage to be authentic.
- **Social:** When we fail to differentiate between relationships and experiences that revive us from those that exhaust. This involves the inclusion of positive and supportive people.
- **Spiritual:** This involves the ability to connect beyond your individual self, to feel a deep sense of belonging and purpose to a cause that is greater than yourself.

Basically, if managers have not included 'rest' within their team's personal development programmes, then they may have failed in their duty of care. That is because such an oversight could set those under their care on a path of completely preventable self-destruction.

One person who mastered rest and concentration was Francesco Cirillo. In the late 1980s, he was enrolled in a university in Rome and became frustrated with his lack of focus due to a tendency to be distracted. To mitigate this, he employed some student resourcefulness by using his tomato-shaped kitchen timer to divide his study sessions into 15-minute blocks. Within these sessions, Cirillo would close himself off to the outside world and concentrate intensely for 10 minutes, immediately followed by a 5-minute rest break.

Soon after employing this strategy, Cirillo noticed a marked improvement in his information retention skills. He ploughed on through his studies, whilst simultaneously perfecting this methodology, and eventually settled on 30 minutes being the optimum pomodoro (25 minutes work/5 minutes rest). Cirillo's solution helped him graduate and then propelled him into management consultancy, where he selflessly named the process the Pomodoro (Tomato) Technique, in honour of the kitchen timer.

The technique has been proven to work for several reasons. By counting down on a timer, as opposed to watching a clock count forward, the technique abstracts time and creates self-induced eustress (beneficial stress). The frequent breaks also ensure a stronger engagement with the subject matter through the prevention of intellectual boredom (preventing procrastination). The breaks also help regulate a healthy psychological load which can sustain a steady cognitive pace for longer periods.

We need to accept the idea that it is unrealistic to expect a person to be always productive throughout the entire working day. It has been proven beyond doubt, within numerous scientifically valid studies, that human concentration works in 'pulses', arguably the most credible of which states a 52-minute/17-minute split is optimum.

I respect that research, and all the effort and work that went into its publication, but I would also add the caveat that we all possess different levels of cognitive ability, and so a manager must find the optimal splits within our daily 8-hour workday sit-a-thons. One theory is that we confuse what is urgency with what is important. Former US President Eisenhower eloquently summed up this concept when he said, 'What is important is seldom urgent and what is urgent is seldom important.'

Eisenhower's words suggest there is rarely a meaningful correlation between what is perceived as urgent, and what is known to be important. This means we cannot necessarily view the relationship as mutually exclusive or interdependent, but more irrational due to a natural tendency to put time-sensitive tasks at the top of the list (regardless of their importance).

The principle behind Eisenhower's words was developed by Dr Stephen Covey in his book *The 7 Habits of Highly Effective People*. Here, Covey set out what he referred to as the Urgent Important Matrix. The purpose of this matrix was to ensure the effective and efficient management of time by prioritising the right tasks, challenging certain habitual behaviours, and reducing needless interruptions and distractions from the workday.

Whilst manager rhetoric usually asks the workforce to 'do more with less', I am not so sure there is a commensurate amount of coaching to facilitate a team to find those fine margins. The Urgent Important Matrix can do that and act as a key enabler in changing a reactive working culture to one with satisfied, healthy, and guilt-free personnel that leave the office with a smile at the end of the working day. So, if you regularly hear 'I am firefighting' when you ask how someone's day is going, why not do them a favour and tell them about a past US President's thoughts on the subject.

In respect of 'do more with less' (now the optime of a cliché), I have a well-worn speech that I roll out at the start of every project and which has evolved over time as the product of a huge amount of career wins, as well as more losses (and lessons) than I would care to mention. One of the subjects that I consistently address in the speech is the triple constraint theory. It always surprises me how many personnel who are allegedly 'project competent' are not familiar with the concept. It centres around the pivotal role played by the project enablers of quality, time, and cost.

According to the Association for Project Management (APM), the definition of project management is, 'The application of processes, methods, skills, knowledge and experience to achieve specific project objectives according to the project acceptance criteria within agreed parameters... constrained to a finite timescale and budget.'

The link is that quality, time, and cost are interdependent, and it is impossible to change any of them without affecting the others. For example, changing the quality of a project will alter the required time and cost, in the same way as a change to cost will impact both time and quality, and time will impact upon both quality and cost.

Therefore, the best project managers are never too far away from a spreadsheet of one form or another. This is not because they like spreadsheets (that is a rare breed), but because the database of figures is used as their playbook to manage each of the three aspects, so that they have a rolling understanding of the changes and concessions that are being made.

Projects are separate from business-as-usual activities, but their principles are transferable and scalable. A project is any endeavour undertaken to achieve objectives, which are defined in terms of outputs, outcomes, or benefits. The degree of granularity within the acceptance criteria that are used to decide whether an objective has been achieved is generally decided by the project manager. However, never forget that every action is dictated by a triple constraint.

The basic premise of the triple constraint is that time, cost and quality dictate decisions. You will find that you only ever have real control of two aspects. This means you could complete something quickly and cheaply, but quality will suffer. Or, you could have good quality and be on time, but that will cost. Lastly, you have high quality and low cost, but that will take time.

In general, everything can be done quicker with more resources, and everything has a cost associated. For me, however, the defining principle is quality, which is often like beauty, and 'in the eye of the beholder' (and so it is often dependent on your client, but ultimately driven by your professional integrity). Time, cost and quality are the building blocks of every project.

There are many different techniques that can be used to control a project schedule and for managing dependencies, change and risks. In today's world, there are many useful software tools, but I have never found one that beats the one that I was taught on: the Gantt Chart.*

This trusty chart is used to map those tasks that can be done in parallel, and those that need to be done sequentially. Once we have defined our scope (which can also be changed), we can consider our resources, costs, and time to produce a 'best fit' schedule to follow. This can be used to gate the process with project milestones, and effectively monitor and report progress.

What sets a project apart, and firmly plants it in the journey from good to great, is the team's ability to accurately risk profile at the logical junctures within the project. A risk profile is an equilibrium that lies between risk tolerance (comfort with volatility), the inbuilt capacity for risk (reserves versus liabilities), and risk requirement (rationale behind the risk proposal).

There are many more aspects to running big projects, from budgetary control to managing stakeholders. However, the most vital is your team. To set up for success, you will need the best experience and knowledge that your resources can buy (a worthy investment), leaving you to

---

* Which can be further enhanced when used in tandem with a precedence diagram, which will identify inter-dependencies, show priorities, and identify the critical path (essential step).

provide the framework and motivation to deliver 'on time and under budget'.

So, this means the quest for motivation and performance is intrinsically linked with how much of an understanding you have in terms of your time, cost, and quality expenditure. In a post-pandemic world, you would do well to ensure that you have a comprehensive understanding of what that equation looks like when laid over the top of your team.

If you don't, legacy traps lay in wait, preying upon our arrogant belief that the 'new ways are the best ways', whilst we ignore the fact that our advancements are founded on legacy thinking. In times gone by, we would blame individuals for negative outcomes, but thankfully we have realised that organisational issues play a more deadly role than any single person ever could.

What follows are several common themes that were said to be in place within the National Aeronautics and Space Administration (NASA) and the Royal Air Force (RAF) at the time of the loss of the Space Shuttle Columbia (2003) and a Nimrod aircraft over Afghanistan (2006). It is not possible to define the extent that these factors may, or may not, have contributed to the outcomes... but that's not the point. The point is to highlight that they were present:

1) Both organisations suffered from 'change fatigue' in the decade that led up to their respective disasters. NASA had created a specific job function to drive an administration transformation; the RAF, on the other hand, had suffered from continual administrative turmoil.

2) The 'McKinsey effect' influenced both organisations. Business principles had been forced upon NASA, with the same happening to the RAF because of the Strategic Defence Review, which saw the introduction of unfamiliar language and methodologies.
3) An insatiable thirst to cut costs and increase efficiency had led to the NASA shuttle workforce being described as 'the few, the tired'. This was also thought to be true of the RAF in 2006, and widely publicised as endemic in the wider British military at the time.
4) Due to cost cutting, NASA had outsourced many critical responsibilities. This meant they had inadvertently eroded their in-house technical expertise. Due to a diminished uniformed workforce, the RAF had done the same and so became reliant on industry.
5) The functions of the NASA Safety Mission and Assurance and the RAF's Airworthiness programmes had been eroded. This resulted in neither providing the independent oversight they had been commissioned for, and they provided little more than compliance audits.
6) Both organisations used dysfunctional information systems that prevented data-driven outcomes. NASA's systems were known to be cumbersome and difficult to use, whilst the RAF's had evolved so much over the years that they were described as incoherent.
7) NASA and the RAF both shared a love for PowerPoint engineering. This was done in place of technical papers, which

detailed the reasoning and analysis that drove decisions. This lack of peer review ensured flawed thinking remained hidden and unchallenged.

8) The culture of both organisations had normalised deviance. In NASA, the engineers had transferred the classification of certain safety concerns into simple maintenance issues, whilst the fuel leaks on the Nimrod were simply thought of as something to tolerate.
9) Due to the amount of time without any notable failures, NASA had fostered the belief that future success could be based on past assumptions. It was highlighted in the Nimrod investigation that the aircraft's successful flight history had influenced the Safety Case.

So, if you find yourself in a high hazard industry and your organisation is: in continual flux; forcing business principles upon technical disciplines; cost cutting resulting in questionable behaviours and unrealistic expectations ('the few, the tired'); contractors fill in-house skills gaps; low oversight with high confidence; problematic/misunderstood information systems; and meetings that are drowned in PowerPoint... then you may want to start asking questions.

It was Henry Ford in 1926 who started the 5-day, 40-hour working week for his assembly line workers. It was necessary at that time; but, 100 years later and (pre-pandemic), we still require people to be in a prescribed place at a required time to do a mandated thing. The difference now (post-pandemic), is that there is overwhelming evidence that there is no threat to production by not all being physically synchronised and tapping our keyboard in unison in office hours.

I welcome positive change and am delighted that the traditional job format appears to be disappearing. Removing the confines of the legacy ball and chain known as ‘the office’, as well as the contractual 5-day sit-a-thon, is a pleasure to behold, and in many cases was a costly and unnecessary expense. The word is out that all the workforce generally needs is a computer, a broadband connection, and a manager who understands the remote workspace.

Research tells us that employees are very committed to this ideal. Research from the World Economic Forum (2021) has revealed that 30% of workers will quit if required to be in an office full time, while a UK YouGov survey finds that 51% of those with a hybrid working agreement would consider leaving their employment if the option were removed.

It is not a surprise that employee experience scores have improved because of the home office. Future Forum have found hybrid and remote employees scoring far better on work-life balance, stress, and work satisfaction than those working full time in an office. This has caused companies, such HSBC’s UK-based business, to reduce office space by around 40%.

Whilst some companies work to reduce footprint, others are creating more attractive and productive environments to encourage collaboration, with breakout areas with state-of-the-art technology. But the physical space is only half the story; the pandemic also highlighted that time could also be flexible, with work completed at 10 am being just as valid as that done at 10 pm.

Data from the United Kingdom's Labour Force Survey (LFS) showed that 391,000 of the 1,020,000 people who left employment from July to September of 2021 had resigned. Before the results were published, most pundits reached for the obvious (Occam's Razor) and stated that the movement was because supply could not meet pandemic recovery demand and so companies hired en masse.

They went on to explain that this immediate injection of life to a depressed labour market sparked fierce competition that left the workforce with options. However, as convincing as that explanation sounds, and whilst leading thinkers and analysts agree that pandemic recovery has a role, there is no consensus on what that influence was.

For example, many believe that being confronted with one's mortality spurred the workforce to reflect on the way they chose to live life. This caused many to rethink spending their finite time with an employer that does not share their values, and redefined employment priorities. Others suggest that, due to people living longer, the workforce has transcended the traditional phase journey (education-work-retirement) in favour of a multi-stage voyage. This caused us to value work which gives us the flexibility to mix and match the different stages.

Of course, there could be many other possible factors. For example, households running on two incomes would result in both parties having less reliance on their respective employer; whilst some built up savings during the pandemic that allowed them to search for greener grass. But, as we try to definitively understand the challenge, what kind of thinking would help lessen the blow of the market readjustment, and perhaps turn it to our advantage? Let's consider the following options:

- Readjust thinking to account for a multi-stage way of working. Ultimately, this means addressing and satisfying your employee's need for flexibility (top of their agenda).

- Accept that the market favours the talent, and that employees know they do not need to 'settle' for questionable cultures, unsociable hours, low pay, poor prospects, etc.

- Open dialogue and be aware of the competition. If a competitor offers something exceptional (particularly involving flexibility), employees will ask why you are not doing the same.

What is certain is that the winners will replace top-down thinking and an MBA approach with active listening, and will look to create a bespoke employee experience that will attract/retain the type of top talent they need in order to dominate their market (a defining leadership quality). Everyone else will take a cookie-cutter approach, and then fight over mediocrity (a defining management quality).

We can see in the market that the companies gaining competitive advantage are attracting top talent with empowerment work cultures that value output over presenteeism. It is in these organisations that innovation is used to build meaningful connections across teams and locations, where everyone has a voice that counts (regardless of whether it is remote or in-person).

This means the winners will be determined by those brave enough to take an informed leap of faith. Unfortunately for everyone else, burying your 'head in the sand' and hoping that, when you eventually emerge, it will be 2019 is not a viable strategy.

In conclusion to this chapter, we should never forget that values really are essential in achieving a vision and to define how an organisation conducts its mission, and that an inclusive and considerate culture plays a huge part in that. Meetings don't always give you what you need. Finally, don't let the misperception of urgent and important combined with the triple constraint lead you down a path of proven disaster.

Final Thoughts

'Life is about making an impact, not making an income.'

—Kevin Kruse

In nuclear physics, a 'half-life' is the time that is required for one-half of the quantity of a radioactive substance to decay. This concept can be used to describe many other workplace processes, from strategy to culture, all of which have decay rates particular to a company.

It is certainly an aspect that needs to be considered when we talk about workforce skills and competence. World Economic Forum research in 2017 found that the half-life of a skill is estimated to be about five years. In 2022, that number was thought to be far closer to four years.

Obviously, there are many facets to this debate. For example, technological skills will likely erode faster than those based on more analogous processes. But, what it does tell us is that there is an impending skill shortage approaching with the potential to cause mass disruption.

This means that, without a significant programme of cross-industry investment in widespread upskilling and/or reskilling of the existing workforce (beyond what academic institutions can offer), we can realistically predict a skills shortfall in the next few years that will result in a semi-permanent talent demand/supply shift away from employers towards employees.

This calls for a fundamental change in organisational philosophy from a 'buy in' to a 'build from within' mentality towards talent. This responsibility does not just fall on the shoulders of organisations; individuals must also realise the value of their professional development and shape it to align with their medium- and long-term visions for their career progression.

In summary, as we move towards Industry 5.0 at a breakneck speed, there is an impending skills shortage. You can either watch it approach and let it wash over you, or take control and manoeuvre yourself into a prime position that will set your career on a planned trajectory. This book will certainly help.

Printed in Great Britain
by Amazon